Studies of Anglophone Literatures in Central Europe

Edited with an Introduction by Wiesław Krajka

Studies of Anglophone Literatures in Central Europe

Bibliographic Information published by the Deutsche Nationalbibliothek
The Deutsche Nationalbibliothek lists this publication in the Deutsche
Nationalbibliografie; detailed bibliographic data is available online at
http://dnb.d-nb.de.

Library of Congress Cataloging-in-Publication Data
A CIP catalog record for this book has been applied for at
the Library of Congress.

This publication was financially supported by
Maria Curie-Skłodowska University, Lublin

Cover image: Courtesy of Benjamin Ben Chaim
Cover Design: © Olaf Gloeckler, Atelier Platen, Friedberg

ISBN 978-3-631-76353-7 (Print)
E-ISBN 978-3-631-77222-5 (E-PDF)
E-ISBN 978-3-631-77223-2 (EPUB)
E-ISBN 978-3-631-77224-9 (MOBI)
DOI 10.3726/b15107

© Peter Lang GmbH
Internationaler Verlag der Wissenschaften
Berlin 2018
All rights reserved.

Peter Lang – Berlin · Bern · Bruxelles · New York ·
Oxford · Warszawa · Wien

This publication has been peer reviewed.

www.peterlang.com

Contents

List of Contributors 7

Wiesław Krajka
Introduction 9

Jacek Wiśniewski
Literary Studies at Polish Universities, 1989–2016: British,
American and Canadian 15

Zdeněk Beran
English Literary Studies in the Czech Republic 47

Olha Bandrovska
Literature of Great Britain and the United States of America
in Contemporary Ukrainian Literary Studies: Scholarly
Accomplishments and Pain Points 61

Soňa Šnircová
Literary Studies in English in Slovakia 75

Madalina Nicolaescu
Managing the Devaluation of English Literature Studies in
Romanian Universities 97

Mirko Jurak, ed. by Igor Maver
Shakespeare's Plays in Slovenia in the First Half of the 20th
Century: The Case of Jakob Kelemina 111

List of Contributors

Olha Bandrovska
Ivan Franko National University of Lviv, Lviv, Ukraine

Zdeněk Beran
Charles University, Prague, The Czech Republic

Mirko Jurak
University of Ljubljana, Ljubljana, Slovenia

Wiesław Krajka
Maria Curie-Skłodowska University, Lublin, Poland

Igor Maver
University of Ljubljana, Ljubljana, Slovenia

Madalina Nicolaescu
University of Bucharest, Bucharest, Romania

Soňa Šnircová
Pavol Jozef Šafárik University, Košice, Slovakia

Jacek Wiśniewski
SWPS University of Social Sciences and Humanities, Warsaw, Poland

Wiesław Krajka

Introduction

The present monograph paints the landscape of studies in Anglophone literatures in five Central European countries: Poland, the Czech Republic, Slovakia, Romania, Slovenia, and one East European country: Ukraine. They outline major trends and achievements in studies of the literatures of the United Kingdom, the United States of America, and of some countries of the former British Commonwealth. It is interesting to see which tendencies in these investigations are common to all these former Communist countries and which are specific to any of them, which ones and to what extent are shared with global research in the field. This publication is an outgrowth of the panel on "English Literary Studies in Central Europe" organized and chaired by professors Wiesław Krajka and Igor Maver within the Triennial Conference of International Association of University Professors of English held at University of London in 2016; most of the articles included here were delivered in their first versions at this conference. Hence, the years 2015 and 2016 are the final caesura for the material covered in these presentations.

The authors of contributions included are distinguished professors and lecturers of Anglophone literatures in their countries: at University of Social Sciences and Humanities in Warsaw (Jacek Wisniewski), Charles University in Prague (Zdeněk Beran), Ivan Franko National University of Lviv (Olha Bandrovska), Pavol Jozef Šafárik University in Košice (Soňa Šnircová), University of Bucharest (Madalina Nicolaescu) and University of Ljubljana (Mirko Jurak).

The material presented in this monograph covers approximately the last century, with concentration on the most recent years: the periods before WW II, from 1939–45 to the "autumn of nations" in 1989, and after that caesura. The middle phase was subdivided in Poland by the political thaw of 1956 which separated her former orthodox Stalinism from later comparatively liberal Communism, and in the Czech Republic by the caesura of "Prague spring" of 1968, followed by political repressions. In this phase Central Europe was largely separated from West European and global studies in literatures in English. However, despite the limitations posed by political factors, intellectual and scholarly activity in this area was thriving, it continued rich intellectual traditions from the former period. In general, the historical-political caesura of 1989 liberated studies in Anglophone literatures in Central Europe (along with other spheres of life) from restrictive ideology and strict political control. It coincided with the split of Czechoslovakia into the Czech Republic and Slovakia in 1993, and with the rising of Ukraine to her independent statehood in 1991, for the first time ever in her history. The essays included in the present book offer multiple perspectives of comparison-and-contrast: of regarding studies in and teaching of literatures in English in a certain country in these three phases (and possibly also in their sub-phases), among the included countries within one phase and in all three phases, as well as of Central European countries and those of Western Europe in all these combinations.

The sequence of the essays follows the types of studies presented: from comprehensive surveys of the entire field of investigations (the contributions on Poland, the Czech Republic, Ukraine, and the first part of one on Slovakia), through evaluative presentation of some of the main and most influential publications (the second part of the latter text), to evaluation of academic system and methods of teaching literatures in English (the essay on Romania) and a sample of literary criticism taken from Slovenia. Thus, the sequence is from synthetic perspectives to monographic ones, focused on definite issues. The texts included reflect rich investigations in this field in the particular countries. This collection does not discriminate against small countries: to render justice to rich critical reflection in Slovenia, a very small country, for which it is impossible to present an extensive survey, it is represented here differently from all the other countries – through a sample of English literary studies conducted there (the abbreviated version the essay written by a deceased colleague, Mirko Jurak, edited by Igor Maver).

The surveys provided by Wiśniewski, Beran, Bandrovska and in the first part of Šnircová's text give valuable information in concise form, and in proportions appropriate to the scope of Anglophone literary studies in these countries. They are solid, informative, comprehensive, selective, and focused on both major tendencies and the particular phenomena illustrating them, and combine manifestations of studies in literatures in English with contexts external to them. They display a variety and wealth of the issues studied, of the critical approaches, schools and areas of research against the changing canon of English literature in the 20th century, especially of contemporary literature. They are arranged by the main institutions which have conducted research in this field and present their major achievements. The contributors discuss investigations in Anglophone literatures centred in English Departments at principal universities and other educational institutions in their countries:

- in Poland: Kraków, Warszawa (Warsaw University, University of Social Sciences and Humanities), Poznań, Lublin (Maria Curie-Skłodowska University, Catholic University), Gdańsk, Wrocław, Łódź, Katowice, Toruń and Olsztyn;
- the Czech Republic, both old ones: Prague (Charles University), Brno, Olomouc, and those opened after 1989 in Prague (Metropolitan University), Ostrava, Hradec Králové, Pardubice, České Budějovice, Plzeň, Ústi nad Labem, Zlin;
- Ukraine: Kiev (National Academy of Sciences, Taras Shevchenko National University, Kyiv State Linguistic University), Oles Honchar Dnipro National University, Zaporizhzhya University, Ivan Franko National University of Lviv;
- Slovakia: Bratislava, Prešov, Nitra, Banská Bystrica, Ružomberok, Trnava (University of Cyril and Methodius, Trnava University), Žilina, Košice.

In Ukraine studies in literatures in English have been positioned as a part of Departments of World Literature, West European Literature, or Foreign Literature. These four surveys cover the whole period in question, with concentration on its last phase (after 1989). Their content and format was neither suggested nor engineered by the editor of the present volume, nor did their authors consult one another on this matter. Despite that, they emerge to be very similar.

These first four articles in the book present most significant monographs, translations, international conferences and other events. Additionally, they view articles (Šnircová), academic journals (Wiśniewski, Beran, Bandrovska), editorial work (Wiśniewski) and developments in related disciplines (for example in translations). All of them cover studies in English literature and American literature. Additionally, Wiśniewski and Šnircová report on investigations in Canadian literature and other Commonwealth and postcolonial literatures. The publications on Anglophone literatures in Poland, the Czech Republic, Ukraine and Slovakia largely share some predominant concerns and methodological approaches practiced in both the United Kingdom and the United States of America. Some of these essays address also the problem of access to major global publications in this area and various forms of support provided by British, American and Canadian institutions.

Monographic treatment of the material starts with the second part of Šnircová's article which gives a fairly detailed insight into some major and most influential publications in this field which represent some mechanisms and frames of thinking behind academic research in Slovakia. Whereas Wiśniewski, Beran and Bandrovska merely enumerate some major works of criticism on literatures in English in their countries, Šnircová both enumerates and briefly discusses select books and articles published in her country. She emphasizes their valuable insights into theory of literature and applications of methodology of literary studies; emphasis on ideological v. aesthetic concerns; positioning vis-à-vis modernism, postmodernism, feminism and gender issues; predominant thematic concerns; and their usefulness for teaching Anglophone literatures at the University level.

All these four surveys give some prominence to the content and structure of wide-ranging teaching programs and courses (both obligatory and optional), as well as to the strategies and mechanisms of teaching literatures in English at the BA, MA and PhD levels. They especially emphasize the opposition of autonomy and freedom v. centrally planned curricula, and structuring and development of the framework of academic teaching in EU countries within the Bologna process. All these issues are of central concern in the contribution on Romania which continues the monographic format of essays initiated by the second part of Šnircová's text. Nicolaescu examines internal and external (transnational) factors shaping the teaching of Anglophone literatures at Romanian universities, especially at University of Bucharest (including her own experiences in teaching Shakespeare there). She asserts that in Romania, unlike in Poland and the Czech Republic, "the attempt to devolve power to departments and chairs has not been very successful and authority and control are still vested with the Ministry," which has resulted in continuation of former teaching strategies and homogeneity of the teaching system, reinforced through application of the Bologna educational frame, openness of higher education to people and its chronical underfunding. Against this landscape Nicolaescu addresses the problem of erosion in scope and importance attached to teaching literatures in English. She claims that this undesirable process has been caused mainly by the paradigm shift in higher education toward its market-oriented vision, and changes in the curricula of secondary school education in English and in the content of final school examinations. According to her, elective courses are a ray of hope amidst this gloomy landscape: they counteract marginalization of study of Anglophone literatures and have a potential to contribute to development of critical spirit and narrative imagination and to relate these studies to Romanian culture. Through illuminating some universal mechanisms of teaching literatures in English in contemporary times Nicolaescu's insights and diagnoses apply to other Central European countries, as well as to many countries outside this geopolitical area.

William Shakespeare is the writer who features most prominently in this volume. Many publications in the Czech Republic and Ukraine concern his literary output, and the last two monographic papers – by Nicolaescu and Jurak – focus on it as well. Nicolaescu examines teaching Shakespeare at Romanian Universities as a case study for her general discussion, and Jurak's contribution is strictly limited to theatrical and translative reception of Shakespeare's plays in Slovenia. He discusses Jakob Kelemina's critical introductions to Shakespeare's plays and evaluative reviews of their translations into Slovenian by Oton Župančič as a sample criticism of reception of his plays in this country in the 1st half of the 20th century and a case study typical of research into English literature there. It is contextualized with a presentation of historical development of drama and theatrical life in Slovenia, and especially of stage adaptations and translations of Shakespeare's plays. Kelemina's interpretation and commentary focuses on the poetic nature of Župančič's translations, rendering Shakespearean evil and some other ethical implications, and the use of Slovenian language in translations. Jurak regards them as important for future theatrical reception and translations of Shakespeare's plays into Slovenian language. Like Nicolaescu, Jurak depicts patterns of reception which are typically Slovenian, pan-European and global. Through relating theatrical reception of Shakespeare's plays in Slovenia to that in other European countries, to contemporary European drama, he also illuminates quite strong ties of the culture of this very small nation with some main trends in European literary and cultural life (mainly in Austria, Germany and England).

Relations of the presented material to its extra-literary contexts, especially political ones, highlighted in all the essays, may be another field of comparison and contrast. Between WW II and the 1989 "autumn of nations" political pressures from the Communist system were present in all these countries. They were the strongest in Ukraine, which was a part of the Soviet Union and gained her independence as late as 1991, and in the Czech Republic where political purges affected Universities and their English Departments after the "Prague spring" of 1968 (hence they are emphasized in the contributions by Beran and Bandrovska); and they were probably the weakest in Slovenia which was a part of Communist Yugoslavia. The reports also imply various strategies of political control used in the countries of Central Europe.

All the studies included here have well-researched and solid basis of facts and data. In the reports by Bandrovska, Nicolaescu, Šnircová and Jurak it is reflected in the footnotes and bibliography of appropriate secondary sources. For Wiśniewski and Nicolaescu it is constituted by reports prepared by Heads of University English Departments compiled prior to writing their articles. Nicolaescu's argument is based also on answers to questionnaires sent by academics teaching these subjects at major Romanian Universities and interviews with students of English Department of Bucharest University. And Beran drew information mainly from web pages of the English Departments in his country.

It is hoped that, owing to the present monograph, studies in Anglophone literatures in Central Europe are no longer a white blank, a terra incognita, on the threshold of the era when they come to stronger integrate with global research in the field.

Lublin, April 2018

Jacek Wiśniewski

Literary Studies at Polish Universities, 1989–2016: British, American and Canadian

Abstract: Since 1989 English literary studies in Poland have undergone a series of significant changes. The Polish Educational Act of 2005 stipulates three stages in the academic programmes of literary studies: BA, MA and PhD studies. There are 16 state universities in all major cities which run full academic programmes in English literary studies (including studies in literatures and cultures of other English-speaking countries); one university, John Paul II Catholic University of Lublin (KUL), is run jointly by the state and the Church; one school, SWPS University of Social Sciences and Humanities, the first private university in Poland with campuses in five cities, acquired the academic status of a university in 2015. Several schools of higher learning and teacher training colleges also run 3-year BA programmes in English; graduates from those schools may continue their education in state and private universities situated in 16 cities throughout Poland. The oldest Polish university is the Jagiellonian University in Cracow (1364); the youngest is the Jan Kochanowski University in Kielce (2011). The first part of this chapter focuses on English literature (British and Postcolonial): I present particular achievements of leading Institutes of English Studies in Poland, regular conference cycles, publishing ventures, continuing exchange programmes, and unique research projects in new areas. In the second part of the chapter, I focus on Literary Studies in Poland – Literatures of Other English-Speaking Countries, on the reception, criticism and teaching of literary works in English produced outside the UK (the US, Canada, Australia, New Zealand, Ireland and others).

Keywords: Polish universities, study of literatures in English, reform in education

It is difficult to describe something that is bigger than Melville's Moby Dick, and perhaps as elusive as that white whale: the development of academic literary studies over the last quarter century in almost a score universities in Poland, covering not only the British (i.e. English, Scottish, Welsh and Irish) aspects, but also other English-speaking countries on several continents (which I will briefly mention in the second part of this chapter, with focus on the United States and Canada, closing with a handful of remarks about Australia, New Zealand, and postcolonial literature). It is hard to provide a fair account of various critical approaches, schools and

tendencies without becoming tedious. The field is vast and various: the no-
tion of the literary canon, still in place three decades ago, is today in serious
retreat; once we admit that we cannot possibly exclude such writers as
Salman Rushdie, Kazuo Ishiguro, Hanif Kureishi or Chimamanda Ngozi
Adichie from our field of study (just because their names sound un-Eng-
lish), we are facing an even more intimidating task.

North to south, and east to west, every Polish county and every major
city has one or two or in some cases three universities where the study
of English language, culture, history, literature and art are conducted at
the BA, MA and PhD level. So, we could start chronologically, with the
oldest, Jagiellonian University in Cracow established in 1364, where lecture rooms and rector's offices are located in splendid Medieval halls; we
could then proceed to the youngest, which happens to be my University of
Social Sciences and Humanities in Warsaw, the first private university in
the country, was awarded a university status in 2015. Another way would
be to present the review geographically, with the central five districts
(those in the middle) discussed first, and then proceed to the eleven around
them. Whichever method we choose, the overview of English/American/
Canadian and postcolonial studies in Poland will clearly show considerable diversity and richness. After 1989 all the established universities
enjoyed relative autonomy and freedom after decades of centrally planned
curricula; several new vocational colleges in provincial towns (teaching at
the BA level) remained for quite some time under the academic supervision
of the well-established older universities, but before long their dynamic
development freed them of that supervision, and today many of them are
aspiring to the status of universities. The first decade after the political
changes introduced in 1989, was the time for educational reforms and
experiments, while ten years later the Bologna Declaration, signed by
twenty-nine Ministers of Education, included Poland in the Bologna process (which there is no need to discuss at length here, because we are all
familiar with its advantages and disadvantages).

In the first part of this chapter I will focus on the development of literary
studies in Poland in reference to the United Kingdom, what is often loosely
referred to as "English" literature, from Beowulf to the present moment.
In the reports which Heads of English Departments from all Polish universities sent to me in preparation for the 2016 IAUPE Conference, mostly by

those Deans and Heads of Departments who remember the situation before 1989, one general note is heard again and again: it acknowledges the tremendous help English Departments received from the British Council in the 1970s and 1980s (and through them, from British universities and individual scholars). We all realised that the decision to terminate the Council's assistance to central European countries after the changes was an inevitable process. Professor Krystyna Stamirowska from the English Department of the University in Kraków (and its former Head) expressed these feelings best when she wrote about the final period of extensive support given to new plans and initiatives. She is referring to the years 1991–1994, when the Director of the British Council was Ian Seaton. The initiatives of that period included the creation of the Polish Association for the Study of English (PASE) and its inclusion in the European Association for the Study of English (ESSE). Professor Stamirowska wrote: "The later policy of the British Council aiming at re-directing their means to the East was understandable but painful to us. The post of a British lecturer and Polish-British projects were closed. There were no finances for academic visitors. The British Council stopped supporting our libraries financially"[1]. In my opinion one unfortunate decision was the dispersal of the magnificent collection of the British Council Library to various colleges, universities and even local libraries in Poland. That collection was something to build upon, but in some cases the decisions about who gets what were a bit haphazard to say the least.

On the other hand, the new Polish currency introduced in 1995, and a relatively steady Polish economy in the early years of the 21st century meant that university libraries (and individual scholars) could afford to buy more books and journals, and get ready access to digital platforms like JSTOR. The same is true about travel to Britain for conferences, summer schools and research stays: in the past it was only possible with a grant-in-aid provided by the British Council or by the Oxford Hospitality Scheme for Polish scholars; today Polish universities have resources of their own for foreign travel grants, research grants,

---

1   Krystyna Stamirowska, "English Studies at Jagiellonian University after World War II", *Institute of English Studies Newsletter* No. 51/ Autumn 2013, p. 13.

for international symposia, summer schools, buying books or paying subscription fees. Greater openness in Europe, and greater freedom of travel means that many more of our students take advantage of exchange programmes (and the presence of many Erasmus students in our universities encourages everyone, teachers and students, to speak English all the time in class); but it is also true that our students now spend more time in Britain or other English-speaking countries, getting first-hand experience of the culture, language and the arts. Some students go to Britain to work over the summer holidays, and some interrupt their studies to spend a whole year or more in Britain or America. From the teachers' point of view this is both good and bad: we are dealing with students who know more about Anglophone cultures, but their course of studies may take much longer.

It is impossible to enumerate here all the exciting international conferences which Polish universities hosted in the period under discussion, 1989–2016. I can only perhaps compare the conferences organized in the 1980s with those which we hosted in recent years (usually in series of annual meetings, of the Polish Association for the Study of English, Polish Association for American Studies, Polish Association for Canadian Studies and Polish Association for Studies of Australasia). In the 1980s, we could only rely on the generosity and cooperation of the British Council to finance the participation of our invited speakers. I remember one conference, a relatively small affair organized by Warsaw University, when we had the pleasure of listening to lectures by David Lodge, Bernard Bergonzi and Barbara Hardy, and attending a film show (with a power cut in the middle of it), and a reading by Ian McEwan (by candlelight). Publishing the proceedings of that conference took years, and today the volume looks like some kind of samizdat pamphlet! Nowadays, each conference (some of them in well-planned series focusing on a particular period, or genre, or theoretical perspective) attracts dozens of scholars from Poland and abroad, offers additional events like poetry readings, excursions, workshops and round table debates. The Jagiellonian University has its *Kraków April Conference* series, as well as *Bloomsday in Kraków*; the Catholic University in Lublin has its *Texts* series; Maria Curie University in the same city is quite famous for its Joseph Conrad conferences; Poznań has its annual *LIES* (Literature in English Symposium), and Warsaw is repeatedly taking a close look at British literature and culture *From Queen Anne to Queen Victoria*. Even the younger and smaller universities like Białystok (travel literature, feminist writing), Olsztyn (translation studies, film studies), Opole (British and American poets of the 20th century), or Rzeszów (postcolonial literature, film adaptation) are doing their best to present the results of their research to the world – I mean conferences, but also published monographs and journals. Institutes of English Studies always respond to an important recent event (migration) or an important anniversary (the Great War and its reflection in literature) with a round of conferences and symposia. Two examples: in 2016 my University of Social Sciences and Humanities in Warsaw organized a Conference *Precarious Places*; in September 2014 Toruń (Copernicus University) hosted a conference entitled *Re-Imagining the First World War: (Hi)stories, Myths, and Propaganda in Anglophone Literature and Culture*. Annual PASE Conferences manage to bring together most of the Polish scholars interested in the study of English literature.

Before I present some of the major academic centres involved in English literary studies in Poland, I must say just a few words about the readers' access to English literature in Poland. We teach English literature in English, and our students read texts in the original, but the majority of Polish readers and theatre goers must rely on translated texts. All the major classic texts are available in translation, with some of them, like all of Shakespeare, translated several times by different translators. I will say nothing about early Shakespearean translations, though some of them still sound fine. In the 20th century all of Shakespeare's plays and all of his poems were published in excellent, and strikingly original translations by Jerzy Sito, Maciej Słomczyński and Stanisław Barańczak, and now in the 21st century, there is a new project by Piotr Kamiński who already translated seven plays (all of them staged in Warsaw), working in a team with a Shakespearean scholar from Warsaw University, Professor Anna Cetera. All the major contemporary writers' work is quickly translated and published in Poland, often becoming bestsellers. For instance, Ian McEwan's novel *The Children Act*, published in Britain in September 2014, was available in Polish bookshops in September 2015. Kazuo Ishiguro's novel, *The Buried Giant*, published in Britain in March 2015, was available in Polish bookshops after just 5 months, published by Albatross Press.[2]

It is important to remember that people teaching and writing about British literature in Poland, those who take part in conferences and publish their work in academic periodicals addressed to fellow academics, are also actively involved in editorial work, in translation of literary texts, poetry, fiction, drama and literary criticism. I only have time to mention very briefly the achievement of one literary magazine, *Literatura na świecie* (or: *World Literature*) which started about forty years ago and is still going strong: nowadays (after the lean years in the 1980s when it was a modest brochure printed on rough paper) it comes in a well bound book-size edition, each issue between 300 and 400 pages long. It has a circulation of several thousand copies and is of course available in all university libraries. The magazine is devoted to the presentation of recent (but sometimes also not so recent) literature in the world to Polish readers. There are essays by Polish scholars, historians and critics, most of them teachers at Polish universities, as well as translations of the most significant texts in literary criticism: essays, interviews with writers, manifestos, letters, new translations of poetry. One example I want to present is last year's issue, 350 pages about British poetry of the 20th century, from Louis MacNeice and Edwin Morgan to Emily Hasler (who I believe is around 30 years old). There are four important essays by Sean O'Brien and Neil Astley, plus a presentation of several women poets. Another example, slightly earlier, from 2012, is very interesting because the whole issue – 450 pages long – prints new translations of Wordsworth, Coleridge, Shelley, Keats and Clare; there are relevant critical essays by Lionel Trilling, Paul de Man, M.H. Abrams and Frank Kermode (but also essays by Polish scholars). Some issues take a close look at earlier periods of English literature: the one with Traherne's name on the cover is a serious reconsideration of Metaphysical Poets, with essays and new translations of poems by Traherne, Herbert and Vaughan. So, the good work of lecturers and academic teachers is one side of the coin, but the

---

2 Information about recent publications of English language writers in Polish can be found at the Polish Society of Authors and Composers (ZAiKS) page, https://online.zaiks.org.pl.

other is their activity as translators, editors, reviewers and literary critics who bring English literature closer to Polish readers.[3]

It is next to impossible to say which Institute of English Studies in Poland is the oldest. Poznań claims to be the oldest, tracing its roots to the English Seminar at Kaiser-Wilhelms-Akademie zu Posen. To be fair, the Polish University of Poznań opened in 1919, and the Department of English was established in 1921, one year before Warsaw, but Warsaw (apart from the war years) is the only state university to boast an uninterrupted activity in Anglophone literatures from 1922 till today – Poznań, like most Polish universities, had a long break in the Stalinist era, when the study of English literature and culture, to say nothing of American or Canadian, was seen by the communist authorities as a dangerous thing. So, they closed down all the Institutes of English, with the exception of Warsaw (where students and staff were closely watched by the authorities), and the Catholic University in Lublin which was the second English Department that functioned in Poland in Stalinist time. The English Department in Warsaw barely survived the 1950s: hounded by officials who insisted on Marxist criticism of the West, it did not manage to educate enough teachers of English (and anyway the main foreign language taught at Polish schools and universities was Russian); our colleagues desperately tried to stay in touch with intellectual trends and ideas in the free world. So in the end, in my opinion, the Jagiellonian University in Kraków has the best claim: their general history goes back to the 14th century, and English studies were first established there in 1911, so English studies at the Jagiellonian University are 106 years old, with just a short break of 6 years during the Stalinist era.

After 1989, with Poland going through a series of radical changes in every field, getting rid of state censorship and control in education, adjusting to market economy and hyperinflation, building up new institutions and carefully dismantling the old ones, education, and particularly teaching foreign languages and cultures became a priority. The demand for teachers of English was so pressing that the Ministry of Education, instead of inflating the existing Departments of English, wisely introduced a scheme

---

3 Information about the monthly *Literatura na Świecie (World Literature)* can be found at www.literaturanaswiecie.art.pl/historia.htm.

which made it possible to open large teacher training colleges in all existing universities, but also in smaller provincial towns. They offered a
3-year BA course of studies, with a possibility of going on to MA at established universities. These colleges all remained under the supervision
of highly qualified university staff, and often employed professors and
lecturers from older universities to teach literature, history or culture. This
means that the number and size of academic institutions in Poland was
suddenly growing in the 1990s. Over the last quarter century these teacher
training colleges managed to assemble and educate its own senior staff,
and – often joining forces with other academic institutions in the vicinity –
to become respectable State Vocational Colleges, or even universities. This
also means that the decade of the 1990s was to many of us the decade of
hard work: during the week teaching in our Departments and continuing
with our research, but over weekends travelling a lot, offering guidance to
the staff of these new colleges, lecturing, examining and supervising PhD
dissertations by ambitious young teachers.

Professor Zygmunt Mazur from the Jagiellonian University in Kraków
(in his report on English studies there) enumerates eight such colleges in
the south of Poland, three of which after a decade became State Vocational
Colleges, perfectly respectable and quite independent institutions of higher
education. Each established university in the country was surrounded by
such a cluster of new colleges.

I want to look more closely at what Professor Mazur says in his historical sketch of English studies in Kraków. He praises the TEMPUS
program, designed not only for teachers of English but also for interpreters
and translators. I should add here that Kraków, Poland's oldest university, excels in several fields of research (Medieval literature, Shakespearean
studies, contemporary British novel); they are also certainly the Polish
leader in the vital field of the theory and practice of translation of literary texts. In this century, they hosted a number of international conferences: the highly regarded *April Conferences* attract scholars from all
over Poland, and also from Britain and the US. In 2005 Kraków hosted
the international conference *Shakespeare: History and Memory* (part
of the international program *Shakespeare in Europe*). A fat volume of
excellent essays was published by the Jagiellonian University Press. Their
evenings of poetry reading with famous British and Irish poets attracted

crowds of students, but also Polish poets (one or two Nobel Prize winners among them), but also translators, publishers and teachers. I remember the exciting moment in 2005 when the Kraków Department of English Literature initiated the procedure of conferring an honorary doctorate on Seamus Heaney (I had the honour of writing one of the reviews). It was very clear to everyone that Heaney, a frequent guest in Kraków, felt very much at home there.[4]

By mid-1990s the Institute of English Studies in Kraków had around 50 staff and 500 students (including extramural courses). I could go on listing their achievements (Professor Mazur's report is 50 pages long!) – of conferences, publications, students' workshops and summer schools, crowned by a very successful conference celebrating the 100 years of English studies in Kraków, but it is time to move north-east to Lublin, which has two excellent universities, the Maria Curie-Skłodowska (State) University, and the Catholic University of Lublin. On the way there, let us notice again the ambitious and growing Department in Rzeszów, which I mentioned before. Comparative literary studies, postcolonial literature, fiction and film studies seem to be their strong points.

English literary studies at Maria Curie-Skłodowska University have a shorter history (compared to Kraków, Poznań and Warsaw) going back to early 1960s, but their achievements are considerable. The Institute of English Studies has about fifty staff, and five Departments dealing with literature and culture of the Anglosphere. Last, but certainly not least, is the unique, world-famous Centre for Conrad Studies, created and headed by Professor Wiesław Krajka, a very good friend of mine whom I sometimes jokingly call the magician of Lublin. The Centre regularly organizes international Joseph Conrad Conferences at Maria Curie-Skłodowska University. In 2016 they finished their Sixth international conference, *Conrad's Footprints*; to the twenty five volumes of essays and studies published in the past, they recently added two more peer-reviewed volumes of the series *Conrad: Eastern and Western Perspectives*, published by Maria Curie University Press in Lublin, and distributed internationally by Columbia University Press (Columbia is Maria Curie's faithful partner

---

4   Zygmunt Mazur, "A Centenary of English Studies at Jagiellonian University, 2011", available at www.ifa.filg.uj.edu/documents.

in this program of Conrad studies). This year's conference, under the honorary patronage of the European Parliament and its President, Mr Martin Schulz, is certainly not the last word in Conrad Studies from Lublin. The Centre also publishes a series of studies about Conrad and his ties to Poland, Europe, and the world (in Polish, all edited by Wiesław Krajka). Traditionally, each Conrad conference ends with a week-long study tour of Conrad's footprints in Poland and (depending on the political situation) in the Ukraine.[5]

I want to add a word more about the Institute in Lublin: I can personally confirm the high academic standard of their publications, conferences and symposia, having reviewed and examined two post-doctoral dissertations and several PhDs., and having participated in several conferences hosted by the Maria Curie-Skłodowska University. Some of my ex-students are now doing research and teaching there. I am impressed by the academic level of their publications (on Dickens, Conrad, Woolf, poets of the Great War, Gerard Manley Hopkins, the early English novel, the Ulster poets). In 2014 Lublin celebrated fifty years of English Studies there with a round of five conferences.

We do not have to move very far to look at another Department of English Literature, just across the street in fact. The Institute of English Studies at the Catholic University of Lublin is one of the oldest and largest in Poland (with around 600 students), though there was no recruitment of students between 1964 and 1982. Very quickly after the Solidarity movement the Department was reopened, and with the help of professors from Kraków and Maria Curie-Skłodowska University, it became an Institute with several unique sections (Celtic Studies, English and Commonwealth Literature) and unique publication series: *Lublin Studies in Celtic Languages and Studies in Literature and Culture* (in short: SILC). The Catholic University of Lublin, or KUL in short (or as students like to call it, COOL) is famous for its publications on Imagism, narratology, philosophy in literature, magic realism, utopian writing and historical romance. More than once, during annual conferences organized by PASE, I was

---

5 More information about Joseph Conrad studies at Maria Curie-Skłodowska University can be found at www.umcs.pl/pl/zaklad-studiow-conradoznawczych,1226.htm.

impressed by the excellent work presented by young scholars interested in the 20th century English novel, Joanna Teske (Virginia Woolf) and Barbara Klonowska (Angela Carter and magic realism).

It takes about two hours by car or coach from Lublin to Warsaw. On the way, we may send our best wishes to our colleagues in the new centres of English studies in Siedlce and Kielce, and wish them luck in developing programmes of study and building up their scholarly structure and reputation. Both are new universities, but this year Siedlce is getting ready for their first international conference on English literature.

My acquaintance with the Warsaw Institute of English Studies is very long. I was a student and a PhD student there, and then I spent something like thirty-five years teaching there, so I can assure you the information contained in Professor Małgorzata Grzegorzewska's report is valid. Two of the five departments at the Institute of English Studies (British Literature and American Literature departments), focus on research and literary criticism. Research in the British Literature Department ranges from Old English literature to the 21st century. Critical approaches include cultural criticism and postcolonial studies, New Historicism and feminist theory; other critical approaches include psychoanalysis, Mikhail Bakhtin, semiotics of culture, memory space and theory of trauma. Notable areas of research comprise the study of Shakespeare in philosophical and theological contexts, the history of his reception in central and eastern Europe, John Milton, the second generation of metaphysical poets including Marvell and Crashaw and the philosophy of language in the 17th century, Renaissance rhetoric and early modern book history. 18th century research areas include Pope, Thomson, Cowper, Ann Radcliffe and women's literature; the great novelists, Richardson, Fielding, Smollett and Sterne, and Polish reception and translations of 18th- and 19th century prose. Explorations in 19th century studies include research into Jane Austen and Romantic writers (notably Coleridge), the connections between literature and the visual arts (Blake), and depictions of women in art and literature. Research on the Victorian period includes studies on Robert Browning, Lord Tennyson, women's poetry, the pre-Raphaelites, Dickens, and Gothic elements in literature. 20th- and 21st century interests focus on narratology, film adaptation, fantasy and science fiction (20th century utopias and dystopias, the New Wave in Great Britain, science fiction and horror stories); the figure and cultural myth of Charles Darwin in popular science, modern novels and mass culture; war literature (poetry, novels, non-fiction); the modernist and post-modernist novel, popular culture in modern prose, the British short story, the Irish novel, and modern British poetry. The Institute organizes a series of conferences *From Queen Anne to Queen Victoria*, biennial international multidisciplinary conferences on British literature and culture in the 18th- and 19th century, and *Scotland in Europe*, a biennial international conference on Scottish culture, literature, identity and languages (there is a rich Scottish studies programme coordinated by Professor Aniela Korzeniowska: my last PhD student at Warsaw University has just finished her dissertation on Scottish women novelists, 1990 – 2010). I will spare you the long list of "notable recent book publications" contained in Professor Grzegorzewska's report, but it certainly confirms Warsaw's standing among major centres of research in Poland. I remember students at the Faculty of Modern Languages in Warsaw saying: we are not the oldest (Kraków is), and we are not the largest (Poznań is), but we are certainly the best.[6]

Now we are looking north or north-west toward the Baltic Sea. Before I say anything about the fascinating things happening at Gdańsk University, just a few more words about Toruń (Copernicus University which was mentioned before) and Olsztyn in the Lake District. Toruń is a lovely old town, but its Department of English Philology is quite young, reactivated after more than thirty years in 1986. Studying there must be fun: the campus is in the very heart of a Medieval town, a mixture of old and new; their library is well stocked, they have exchange programmes with eight European universities, and they have their own student theatre, The Spinning Globe. Their teachers are very active in PASE, but they also run their own conference series (I mentioned one of them earlier). I will say more about their Centre for Canadian Studies in the second part of this report. Olsztyn started recruiting students in 1999. Their Faculty of Humanities (which includes the Department of English) organized two conferences already (translation studies and film studies); their scholars are into popular literature, Gothic literature and fantasy.

---

6   More information about English studies at Warsaw University can be found at
     www.ia.uw.edu.pl/en/about-the-institute/history.

Gdańsk (here I rely on the information provided by Professor Jean Ward, deputy director of the Institute there): the Institute of English and American Studies is only four years old, but earlier it existed as a smaller Department of English Philology. Its four main sections are English and American literature, culture and linguistics. Its newest section is the Chair of Drama, headed by Professor Jerzy Limon, the moving spirit behind the construction (or rather re-construction) of the Gdańsk Shakespearean Theatre. Gdańsk is also a leading centre of translation theory and practice: taking advantage of the presence of several British scholars, some of whom are also creative writers and poets, they promote co-translation as a means of achieving the best results in literary translation. One example among many: Olga and Wojciech Kubińscy, working with a visiting scholar from Newcastle University, Professor Desmond Graham, produced a series of translations of Anna Kamieńska and Julia Hartwig's poems. They also translated quite a number of poems by Graham, some of which are about Poland after the fall of the Berlin wall. Professor David Malcolm, an expert on recent British novel, is also a translator: with Polish co-translators he produced a series of magnificent translations of Julian Tuwim, one of the most difficult poets to translate. Gdańsk publishes its own journal, *Beyond Philology*; they have their own English language theatre; their series of monographs, *Transatlantic Studies in British and North American Culture*, edited by Professor Marek Wilczyński, is published by Peter Lang (more than a dozen books have been published); their annual festival of literature and theatre, called *between.pomiędzy*, has been tremendously successful. 2014 was rich in interesting developments: the International Byron Society conference took place in Gdańsk. In the same year the Polish Society for the Study of European Romanticisms started its cooperation with "Romantic" societies from European and American Universities.

From Gdańsk, we shall be moving south all the way: to Poznań, Łódź and Wrocław. Our last stop will be in Silesia, bringing us very close to where we started – it is about 50 miles from Katowice to Kraków.

The Poznań School of English (Adam Mickiewicz University) made continued efforts over a number of years to become an independent faculty. They succeeded in 2011. They are certainly the largest school of English in Poland, with 170 staff, 1400 students and 80 participants in PhD programmes. Without a doubt, following in the footsteps of

Professor Jacek Fisiak, probably Poland's greatest English linguist, the Faculty of English is the leading centre for research into various fields of language study; their Centre for Speech and Language Processing and their Language and Communications Lab enjoy the highest reputation; their cyclical international conference series are very well attended (this includes the eleven LIES, or eleven Literature in English Symposia which I mentioned before); their journals are listed in the European Reference Index for the Humanities and are steadily increasing their impact factor; the *Poznań Studies in Contemporary Linguistics* holds first place among Polish linguistic journals.

All this does not mean that literary studies are neglected in Poznań. Generations of Polish students read histories of English literature, first by Professor Henryk Zbierski (who also produced incisive studies of Shakespearean drama); his survey of English literature, 1982, was written in Polish, aimed at all Polish students of the humanities. Then there was Professor Liliana Sikorska's *An Outline History of English Literature*, first published in 1996; its 4th enlarged and updated edition appeared in 2011. Polish students also use the Poznań *Anthology of English Literature* in 2 fat volumes, with extensive notes on literary periods and authors, edited by Sikorska and Fabiszak. But Poznań is also very active in developing Celtic studies, South African studies, Canadian studies, while more programmes are in preparation, e.g. Australia and New Zealand – literature, culture, language. Poznań is the first Faculty of English in Poland where all research activity and teaching takes place in English, so they are ready to become a truly cosmopolitan School of English.

The official Łódź University page has little to say about the achievements of scholars doing research on English literature – it just mentions briefly the Department of American studies and its founder (until recently its head), Professor Agnieszka Salska, whose many publications I will list in the second part of this chapter. And yet the Institute of English Studies in Łódź has an interesting and original structure: they have two Departments dealing with English literature – the Department of British Literature and Culture, headed by Professor Jerzy Jarniewicz, and the Department of Studies in Drama and pre-1800 English Literature, headed by Professor Jadwiga Uchman. Jerzy Jarniewicz is not only a scholar, author of a dozen books, but also a poet, a translator, one of the editors of *Literatura na świecie*, the monthly magazine which I mentioned earlier. His excellent work on British and Irish poets after the Second War goes hand in hand with his many translations of their verse. I had the pleasure of reviewing his post-doctoral dissertation, *Ekphrasis in the Poetry of Derek Mahon* (2013) and I can assure you it is an eye-opening study. Two more years (2014–2015), two more books! One is a collection of essays on Irish Poets, the other (in Polish) is about the art of translating poetry. Jadwiga Uchman specializes in modern drama: Beckett, Stoppard, Pinter. Her long list of publications includes three books about these three playwrights, but she also published essays on Dylan Thomas, T.S. Eliot and Sławomir Mrożek. The Łódź newsletter for June 2016 carries news about *Shakespeare 400*, commemorating the 400th anniversary of the Bard's death. There were lectures by eminent professors from several universities in Poland, Britain and the US; there was a symposium hosted by the International Shakespeare Studies Centre and the Department of Drama; there were workshops for students, and a performance of *A Midsummer Night's Dream* which attempted to recreate the original experience of comedy on the Elizabethan stage.

Our penultimate stop is Wrocław. The University there continues the traditions of the Polish University in Lviv/Lwów/Lemberg (in 1945 the staff of that university were moved to Wrocław), but of course Wrocław University (or Vratislavia or Breslau) has centuries of earlier history behind it, with Czech and German influences, and the University there goes back to the 17th century. The Institute of English is today a very important centre for the study of literature in English, though in the 21st century the Department of Literature was rather small, and had to rely on outside help, and the expertise of scholars from other Polish universities (Professor Krajka is a good example, leading the team of Wrocław scholars for something like thirteen years, commuting between Lublin and Wrocław, teaching, examining, advising and supervising). Young scholars there worked very hard in the early years of the century: twelve teachers got their PhDs, and in the last ten years six of them went on to publish their post-doctoral work, qualifying them for the posts of associate professors. Their report sent to me in the spring 2016 included a list of two dozen book-length monographs on British and American literature (half of them published locally, by Wrocław University Press, and the other half by academic presses and publishing houses abroad). They include volumes devoted to the analysis of one writer's work (John Donne, T.S. Eliot, Samuel Beckett, C.S. Lewis, Kazuo Ishiguro); others approach literary texts created in different epochs from the perspective of feminist criticism, or discuss various modes of autobiographical writing, or travel writing, and examine particular motifs in literature, for instance the figure of the double, or the Doppelganger. Apart from traditional departments dealing with British or North American literatures (both the US and Canada), they also have several smaller Centres with interest in particular periods or issues: the Centre for 19th and 20th century English Literature, the Centre for Young People's Literature and Culture, the Centre for Gender Studies, as well as the Centre for Contemporary American and Canadian Poetry. Apart from the twenty-four single-author monographs mentioned earlier, they published seventeen collections of essays, and proceedings of international conferences organized by the Wrocław Institute. They ran three PASE conferences in 1999, 2008 and 2015 (with 180 participants, discussing the subject of *Emotion(s) in Literature*), and several more in the last fifteen years: on fantasy and SF, literature for children, the anniversary of the Great War in 2014. Their Centre for Postcolonial studies is only eight years old, but it has already started working together with colleagues at Warwick University (it is perhaps worth adding that Wrocław started its cooperation with Warwick University in 1982, then it hibernated in the years when the British Council withheld their financial support of the project, to be revived last year – with European funds).

Our last stop is the Silesian University, with departments in two cities, Katowice and Sosnowiec. The Institute of English Cultures and Literatures is in Sosnowiec, in a lovely new building which is the envy of other universities. People living in Silesia are reputed to be hard working and reliable, but they are very modest when you ask them about their accomplishments. Their report sent to me in December 2015 (typically, they were the first to respond to my enquiry), entitled *Interdisciplinary Studies in the Context of British Culture and Literature*, is comprehensive and very detailed in listing their research subjects and theoretical approaches, but it does not name names, or enumerate titles of publications which are many. I managed to find out that in May 2016 they elected their new head, Professor Zbigniew Białas, an expert on postcolonialism and travel literature; his book *Mapping Wild Gardens* had been selected as the best *Habilschrift* published by Essen University in 1997. Białas is also a novelist and translator of British and American fiction. His *Sosnowiec Trilogy* (2011–2015) received many prestigious prizes. I was impressed by a detailed description of the research conducted by literary scholars in Sosnowiec. They cover all the major periods in the history of English literature; quite apart from the historical take on literary works, they investigate theoretical, cultural, philosophical and structural aspects; among examples provided by their report, I want to mention two: the first is the role of time and temporality in culture and literature. The second example is their focus on the reception and translation of British literature in Polish culture. The students of the Institute of English Cultures and Literatures are very proud of their creative writing programme and the *Writing Centre Magazine*, first published in 2016.

* * * * *

In Poland, every major university has its Faculty of Modern Languages, with Institutes of English Studies which cover quite a range of topics in literature, art, culture, linguistics, methodology of teaching English as a foreign language, translation studies, and many more. In every Institute a very important Department is always American Literature and Culture, teaching also American history, courses in American civilization, politics, popular art, theatre, music and film. I remember when I was a student at Warsaw University a long time ago, only the very best students, with the highest grade average, could get into seminars on British literature, with American literature an obvious second choice. Ten years later the situation was reversed, reflecting perhaps the tremendous pull which the incredible reality of America (as described by Bernard Bergonzi in the 1970s) exerted on Polish students of English. Soon these Departments of American Literature set up independent study units called American Study Centers. Until fairly recently, the same teachers and scholars were offering lectures, classes and courses in both: the Departments of American Literature within the Faculty of Modern Languages, but also in American Study Centers. With the passage of time, and especially in the period we are looking at, after 1989, American Study Centers became more and more interested in politics, law, society and business, while Departments of American Literature remained faithful to *belles lettres*. On the whole, it is impossible to talk about literary studies in

Poland which focus on American literature without considering both types of academic institutions. Fortunately, very soon all these ventures were smoothly incorporated into the Polish Association for American Studies, PAAS, with its excellent publishing programme, its links with the European Association for American Studies, and its rich calendar of conferences.

The Polish Association for American Studies (PAAS), its development and achievements in the last twenty years or so, can be best seen if you take a look at their Newsletters, available online since 1995. The newsletter for 1995, covered just eight modest pages. It listed new publications, forthcoming conferences, and calls for papers. Twenty years later, the newsletter for 2015, with similar content, is fifty pages long: the list of publications in Polish and foreign journals is much longer; the list of forthcoming conferences consists of fifteen items, and on top of all this there are also calls for papers by several international conferences organized abroad. New items include lists of guest lectures, exchange programmes, and a list of publications by Polish scholars in American journals. What is more, in recent years the PAAS newsletter prints news from fifteen academic Centers of American studies, while twenty years ago there were only five of them in existence.[7]

The newsletter lists all conferences, guest lectures and publications; some are events open to faculty and students, like *Narration and Storytelling*, a Second Student Symposium organized in March 2015 by Adam Mickiewicz University in Poznań. Others are international gatherings of scholars, like *The aesthetics and politics of contemporary women's life – writing in Canada and the US*, organized in the same month, March 2015, and in the same city. Two months later, in May 2015 there was the 11th Literature in English Symposium (nicknamed LIES), this time devoted to *Poetry and Beyond*; keynote speakers were Paul Muldoon and Nick Hayes (again in Poznań). This is just one example from one university. Other events were taking place from Białowieża in the east to Szczecin in the west.

Academic exchange programmes with American universities, learned societies and foundations provide interesting opportunities for Polish scholars to study and lecture abroad, and for American teachers to lecture

---

7   All PAAS newsletters between 1995 and 2017 (in PDF) can be accessed at www. paas.org.pl/newsletter/.

in Polish universities and Centers for American Studies. Our colleagues returning after a semester or two are always full of interesting ideas for new courses and lecture series. Jerzy Durczak, a professor at the Maria Curie-Skłodowska University, and his wife, Professor Joanna Durczak, started four innovative courses after their recent stay in the US: Jerzy Durczak – *Politics and American Literature and Cult Literature* and *Film*; Joanna Durczak – *Americans and the Environment,* and *The Environmental Imagination.* Again, this is just one example among many.

The American Studies Center at the University of Warsaw (established already in the 1970s) is one of the biggest American Studies departments in Europe. It employs over twenty faculty from Poland and the US, and provides excellent research facilities for students, scholars and professionals interested in the field. The American Studies Center Library is the largest American Studies library in Central Europe, containing a sizable microfiche and microfilm collection, and a wide array of recent academic publications. The Center for American Studies at the Jagiellonian University was set up in March 1991 and is located in the very heart of Cracow's historic centre. The permanent staff of the Center is rather small, but it cooperates with several professors from outside the Center whose research interests focus on North American issues. Among them there are historians, sociologists, lawyers, economists, political scientists, specialists in American literature, and art.

As I mentioned at the beginning of this chapter, a lot can be learnt about American literary studies in Poland from a review of the PAAS newsletters. Members of the Association are frequent speakers at conferences organized by British, Scandinavian, Austrian, French and German Associations of American Studies, and perhaps less frequently, at conferences in the US. Most Polish scholars interested in American studies regularly visit and study at the John Fitzgerald Kennedy (JFK) Institute of American Studies in Berlin. Berlin also organizes workshops and consultations for PhD candidates; it seems such a perfect idea and a convenient venue: American scholars who visit the JFK Institute are willing to find the time for discussions and consultations, and Berlin is just five hours away by train from Warsaw!

I should say something about the role of several American institutions which offer grants and scholarships to Polish scholars – their role is similar to what in the past was taken care of by the British Council and the British Embassy in relation to English studies. First of all, the Polish-US Fulbright Commission, regularly offering Fulbright grants in American Studies to young Polish scholars. A similar programme is also the good work of the Kościuszko Foundation and the American Council of Learned Societies – without their help the achievements of Polish Americanists would not be the same. The Mellon Foundation was very active, especially in the 1990s, in bringing new information technology to American Studies Centers in Poland, providing funds, know-how and equipment.

Around 1995, Polish scholars interested in American culture started offering courses in popular arts (science fiction and fantasy, film, TV and other media, American painting and other visual arts, American music) during summer schools organized at the Warsaw Center. Courses included: literature by ethnic minority writers; feminist writers; migration, assimilation and multiculturalism; American literature of war in the 20th century; translation of American literature into Polish (with special stress on texts which remain unknown to the Polish reader).

Since the mid-1990s American Studies Conferences (organized by Poznań, Łódź, Warsaw and Cracow) have become regular, annual gatherings of scholars. About twenty years from the moment the first American Studies Center was founded (a joint effort of Warsaw University and Indiana University), i.e. around 1997, American Studies in Poland may be said to have grown up: there were Centers in every major university in Poland, there were regular series of annual conferences, there were *Journals for American Studies* and many other publications, like proceedings of conferences, PhD and post-PhD dissertations; there is *The Americanist*, a Warsaw journal for the study of the United States, a continuation of the series which started out in the 1980s as *American Studies Journal*; there is *AD American: Journal of American Studies* published in Kraków (the most recent issue is focused on American Mythology); the American Studies and Mass Media Department at Łódź University has an impressive list of books, monographs and collections of essays published by their University Press, but recently also in Britain, Germany and the US. Examples include: American film, gender and ethnic identities, migration, assimilation and multiculturalism, national identity and citizenship, representing gender in different cultures, and mass media.

From the end of the 1990s till today, more and more universities in Poland started offering new courses of study and recruiting students for BA and MA programmes in American studies. While it is true that the Centers in Poznań, Lublin, Łódź, Warsaw and Kraków were already well established, the younger universities often relied on visiting scholars and lecturers employed on part-time basis from older universities. After about twenty years of this practice, the smaller universities (e.g. Białystok, Opole) can now boast quite a large staff of PhDs, assistant professors and associate professors of their own. Teachers from Łódź and Poznań often taught courses in several new universities and teacher training colleges, while scholars from the Warsaw Center went all around the country, giving lectures, offering courses, and helping to build up the local initiatives by supervising theses, reviewing, examining and so on.

Polish scholars interested in American studies are a close-knit community, which is the achievement of the vitality and vigour of the PAAS. A typical PAAS annual conference at the beginning of this century attracted about a hundred scholars from a dozen countries, with around fifty papers read and discussed in several sections. Apart from regular annual conferences, individual regional centres also organized workshops, seminars and summer schools devoted to particular current subjects: American film industry, Gothic fiction, Camp, apocalyptic fiction, fantasy and science fiction. Such meetings were always great opportunities to meet and listen to famous critics like Ihab Hassan, Tony Tanner, Judith Butler or David Lehman, and intriguing writers like Harry Matthews or John Irving.

Many more specialized courses were taught before the end of the 1990s: American short story writers, science fiction and fantasy, native American literature, American postmodernism, environmental issues in American literature, the American dream. Some of these specialized courses were offered by Polish scholars returning from the US, and others were offered by Fulbright scholars visiting PAAS Centers (20th century American poetry and drama, American poetry and time, contemporary American critical theory, American western, American civil society).

Even before the 20th century ended, Polish scholars writing and lecturing about American literature began discovering new fields and new possibilities. One international conference focused on postmodern ethics, others discussed new directions in Black studies, Jewish American writing, gender and American women writers; the 1999 annual convention of Polish Americanists explored continuities and fluctuations of the sense of America's special destiny, its spiritual and civilizational mission, its concerns with catastrophic upheavals and self-destructive urges (December 1999, Łódź).

The 2000 Conference in Toruń called for papers on *The Local Colors of Stars and Stripes*, while the Lublin workshop/seminar in the same year focused on the presence and role of visual arts in teaching American Studies. Łódź scholars convened a series of meetings and seminars devoted to multiculturalism in the USA, while Poznań was busy discussing and re-interpreting classic texts: Melville, Emerson, Poe, Dickinson, Faulkner, Frost.

In the first year of the new millennium there were already ten well established Centers of American Studies in Poland. All of them participated in and contributed to a series of conferences. Each of them brought together American scholars from Polish universities and from abroad, the US, Germany, Italy, Holland and Scandinavia. A new note was introduced when the Warsaw Center started teaching a course in gay writing and queer theory. The Interdisciplinary Gender Studies Group at the University of Wrocław was quickly followed by other universities in other cities, bringing together literary critics, historians, philosophers, sociologists and performance artists. Wrocław was also leading the way in postcolonial studies: scholars from Wrocław joined an international team designing a colonial and postcolonial literature syllabus to be used across the European Union.

The University of Silesia is very active in publishing a series of volumes printing essays on *Great Themes in American Literature*, while the new university in the east, Białystok, published a series of three collections of essays on women writers in America, edited by a colleague of mine at the SWPS University, Professor Lucyna Aleksandrowicz. Each year brings a new range of topics and preoccupations: American culture in the era of globalization, ethnicity and gender, literature and culture of the American south, the fight against terrorism. In the period after 9/11 (understandably) quite a number of papers and essays about America used the word Apocalypse in their titles.

The new edition of the Polish Great Encyclopedia (2002) printed a large number of entries on American writers authored by our colleagues from several universities. Theory and practice of translating literary texts was becoming (in a series of courses, conferences and publications) a regular feature, with young translators looking not only at recent American literature, but also coming forward with new translations of classic texts from the 19th and 20th centuries (Eliot, James, Hemingway, Frost and others).

About twelve years ago Polish scholars started appearing as advisory members of boards in European academic societies, and lecturing on American literature and culture in other Eastern/Central European universities (the Ukraine, Hungary, Lithuania, Estonia). Peter Lang Scientific Publications started a new series *American Studies and Media,* with Polish scholars as general editors. In 2004 the first Erasmus exchange agreement was signed by the JFK Institute in Berlin and Warsaw University. The number of Polish universities running BA and MA programs in American studies grew to fourteen. Interesting new topics for conferences organized by those Centers started appearing: the American city, science fiction studies, religion in American literature and culture, travel writing, Asian American writers, etc. In the last ten years or so it is fair to say that American Literature Departments went on with their chief task which was to study and teach literature and culture, while American Studies Centers concentrated more on politics, economy and social matters. This naturally meant that our colleagues teaching in ASCs often appeared as experts and commentators in the Polish media. The number of conferences organized by Departments of American Literature and American Studies Centers was steadily growing; large American Studies conferences were not always attractive to people interested in narrower, particular aspects of American culture and/or history. Instead, smaller gatherings appeared, with scholars discussing for instance American poetry of the 1920s, Gothic literature, poetry by American women, internet resources for American Studies, Cold War America, magical realism in American literature, and so on.

In 2004 the Polish Association for Canadian Studies (in short, PACS) was three years old, old enough to set up its own programmes and journals, and become an independent body; it joined the International Conference of Central European Canadianists; I shall say more about Canadian Studies in Poland later on in this text.

A significant achievement of 2004 was the publication (in two massive volumes) of *Historia Literatury Amerykańskiej XX w. (History of American Literature of the 20th century).* It is the joint effort of ten scholars from several universities, building upon earlier achievements of scholars from Poznań. There is no time to discuss its contents fully, or provide the full list of distinguished authors (the two volumes are almost 1500 pages long!) This of course is not the only or the first history of American literature published in Poland, and I should perhaps mention a 6-volume series of *Great Themes in American Literature* published by Silesian University (volume #6, published in 2014, is entitled *Old Age and Death*). Earlier volumes discussed Religion, The Frontier, The Journey, American cities, American family.

More and more often before the end of the first decade of the 21st century books by Polish scholars started appearing in international publishing houses like Peter Lang (in Hamburg), or Cambridge Scholars Publishing (in Newcastle). Around 2005, many American Studies conferences were co-sponsored by Polish and American universities working together, and several of our colleagues were chosen to co-edit internet journals. Many of our colleagues teaching literature and publishing scholarly papers are also creative writers, publishing their own poetry or volumes of poetry translated from English; others write plays, novels, or translate literary essays which are published in Polish literary journals, and publish critical essays and reviews, to bring the literature of the Anglosphere closer to the Polish reader.

In the last ten years the list of Centers of American Studies at Polish universities (and American Literature Departments) has been getting longer, reaching fifteen in 2015; the list of publications, too, not to mention lists of Conferences, guest lecturers and exchange programs. *Polish Journal for American Studies*, started in 2004, reaches volume number ten this year, and the waiting list for publication is getting longer and longer. Many new courses are offered, some of them online, offered in cooperation with American universities and colleges. Our colleagues attend conferences in the US as often as they can, but they also read papers at conferences organized east of Poland, from the Ukraine and Belorussia, all the way to China and Japan. The new Socrates/Erasmus Teaching Staff Mobility Program made things easier for guest lecturers from abroad and Polish scholars teaching abroad. More and more centres use e-learning and electronic platforms like BLACKBOARD.

In 2006 PAAS started publishing online syllabuses for new courses; listing internet sites for the *European Journal of American Studies* where essays and reviews by Polish scholars regularly appear. In 2007 the first essays started appearing which include critical appreciations of early 21st century literature in the US; and for the first time, courses in Mexican American literature are offered, as well as courses in the history of American painting, American television, the Pentagon, queer film and media, etc. In 2008 colleagues from the Poznań Department of American Literature helped organize workshops in traditional American folk music and singing styles, and several new courses were added to the Department's offer: Jewish American autobiographical writing, American literatures of the fantastic, European influences on American art. 2009 saw new centres opening in independent colleges and private universities in Poland. Those new centres joined the PAAS and hosted several interesting conferences (Collegium Civitas in Warsaw, and the University of Social Sciences and Humanities with branches in five cities). 2010 was the year for student conferences, student Studies Circles and summer schools. For example, the Catholic University of Lublin organized the 1st student conference *American Dream in the 21st century*; and, in collaboration with Maria Curie-Skłodowska University in the same city organized *The International Pynchon Week*. New approaches to American literature included ecocriticism, kidult literature, and the precariat. In the same year a new series in American studies was announced, *American Studies and Media*, in collaboration with Peter Lang Publishers.

In 2011 and 2012 more new voices were heard from new universities and colleges. The staff in those universities and teacher training colleges are young people whose commitment is hard to match. They organize workshops, summer schools and conferences, and run their own publication series with original and challenging topics. One such example is the University in Rzeszów (postcolonial studies), another in Białystok (literature by women). In those years the University of Warsaw also launched a new book series in American literary studies called *Masters of American Literature* (in Polish).

In 2013 several publications and/or conferences focused on postcolonial literature; on race, ethnicity and migration; on the theory and practice of film and TV adaptations of classic texts of American literature. In the same year, the PAAS Newsletter recorded the first conferences and publications by my colleagues in the SWPS University in Warsaw.

In 2014, predictably, there were several conferences, symposia and publications about literature of war in the context of the anniversary of the First World War, discussing memory and commemoration, history and historicity in literature and culture, e.g. *Re-Imagining the First World War: Histories, Myths and Propaganda*, organized by the Copernicus University in Toruń (published in 2015 by Cambridge Scholars). There were also other international conferences and symposia organized by Polish Centers, discussing Music and Literature, Literature and Medicine, Food and Culture, Ethnicity and Literature, Authenticity and Imitation in Literature, Nostalgia in Literature, Borderlands and Wild Zones in Literature, Grief in Literature, Literature and Film, Literature and TV – so much to choose from!

Last year's PAAS Newsletter (October 2015) shows the range and variety of research: it records the activities of fifteen academic institutions involved in American studies; we get fifty pages of events and activities (including a lecture by Professor Thomas Austenfeld of the University of Fribourg, *Robert Lowell and the History of Poetic self-Revelation* – in the Distinguished Professors' Lecture Series in Poznań). We get a long list of conferences, most of them annual events. There is another long list of publications (both in Polish and frequently in foreign university presses), and finally, a list of new courses in American Studies offered by Polish universities at the BA, MA, and PhD level.

* * * * *

The history of Canadian Studies in Poland starts with a number of enthusiastic scholars, who – while working in other, though often related disciplines – engaged in Canada-related research and introduced the Canadian component into their classes. As a result, by the beginning of the 1990s quite a few Canada-focused or Quebec-focused courses were offered in several university centres all around Poland. Today, the fields represented by the majority of the Polish Canadianist community reflect the interests of these first enthusiasts: literature, history, political science and sociology. In the past two decades more universities started to teach Canada-related courses, and several Canadian Studies Centres have been established all over Poland. In 1998 the enthusiasm of Polish Canadianists resulted in the foundation of the Polish Association for Canadian Studies (PACS) – a body which coordinates and provides information on Canadian studies in Poland.

The first Canadian Studies Centre in Poland was established at the University of Warsaw, by scholars interested in French-Canadian Culture and Quebec Literature, in 1982. This was quickly followed by another Canadian Studies Centre (this time focused on literature in English). It was opened in 1994 at the Institute of English Studies, Warsaw University. The idea of the centre was first devised by Professor Nancy Burke, a Canadian poet and scholar, professor of literature at the University of Warsaw, who actively contributed to its creation and was director of the Centre till her death in 2006. Through her Canadian literature courses at the University of Warsaw she was instrumental in shaping the careers of numerous doctoral students, academics, translators and poets. Her knowledge, her energy, her devotion to the study of Canadian literature inspired the beginning of Canadian studies in Poland and the foundation of the Polish Association for Canadian Studies.

While Warsaw University was the first and most active Polish academic centre promoting the study of Canadian literature, the Jagiellonian University in Kraków has been the leader in the study of the history, culture and society of Canada. The Chair of Canadian Studies constitutes today part of the Institute of American Studies. In 1999 a Canadian Studies Centre was founded at the Philology Department of the Copernicus University in Toruń. The Centre is the only one that brings together English and French-Canadian literature specialists and linguists. In 2002 it organized the second PACS conference entitled *Exploring Canadian Identities* and published selected conference proceedings. The previous President of the Association, Professor Mirosława Buchholtz, is one of the few experts in children's and youth literature in the region. Apart from coordinating the activities of the Centre and organizing many events in recent years, Professor Buchholtz is also the general editor of the only "Canadiana" series in Poland. Another scholar engaged in the activities of the Centre, and the present President of the Association, Professor Anna Branach-Kallas, focuses in her research on ethnic and racial minority writers. She published, among others, a monograph *In the Wirlpool of the*

Past: Memory, Intertextuality and History in 2003, and co-edited, with Piotr Sadkowski, a collection of articles on *Dialogues with Traditions in Canadian Literatures* (2005).[8]

The University of Silesia holds a major event organized in Poland each year – *Days of Canadian Culture*. This interdisciplinary symposium aims at exploring and celebrating the uniqueness, complexity and diversity of Canadian culture. The event is a great opportunity for Polish academics, students and the general public to attend lectures, presentations, performances and film shows. The most recent event in 2007 gathered many First Nations scholars, artists and activists who addressed cultural, literary as well as social and political issues of vital importance to First Nations communities.

Canadian literature and culture courses have also been taught in the Department of English in Poznań since the late 1980s. Currently, the Department offers regularly MA seminars on contemporary Canadian literature. Apart from the above mentioned major Canadian Studies Centres, courses in a variety of Canadian topics are also taught in Lublin, Łódź, Bydgoszcz, Konin, and at several other universities and colleges. In 1998 Polish Canadianists organized the First Congress of Canadian Studies in Poland at the University of Warsaw.

PACS organizes triennial congresses, which have successfully served as forums of scholarly debate on Canada-related issues and on the condition of Canadian studies in Poland. These are international events, gathering also experts from abroad, though the majority of the participants are always Polish. The Kraków conference in 2004 examined the complexity of the notions of place and memory in various Canadian discourses. It was a huge event, attended by 160 scholars from all over the world; 100 papers were presented. Conference debates were summarized in the extensive volume of selected conference proceedings entitled: *Place and Memory in Canada: Global Perspectives*.

The 2007 PACS conference was dedicated to exploring the continuities between Canada's past and present. The interdisciplinary nature of the conference attracted many contributors from a variety of scholarly

---

8   All PACS newsletters between 2001 and 2015 can be accessed at www.ptbk. org.pl/Newsletters,45.html.

disciplines, such as history, sociology, law, political sciences, literature and film studies. The 5th Congress of the Polish Association for Canadian Studies, *Towards Critical Multiculturalism*, took place in October 2010 in Kraków. The main theme was Canadian policy of multiculturalism, implemented in 1971, and particularly its origins, determinants and consequences. The 7th Congress – *Canada at war* took place in May 2016 at the Copernicus University in Toruń. It focused on how the tension between Canada as a peacekeeping nation and Canada as a warrior nation is reflected in historiography, politics, literature, film, visual arts, and other cultural discourses.

Today PACS is a successful and dynamic organization. The Association has over one hundred members, and the membership in the Association is constantly growing. The interests and research done by the scholars and students belonging to PACS cover a great variety of scholarly disciplines. Canadian literature remains a dominant discipline, but among PACS members one can also find experts on Canadian theatre, cinema and the media, Native issues, environmental issues, Canadian history and literature (both in French and in English), political sciences, linguistics, sociology, culture and identity studies, gender and immigration studies.

Each year PACS awards the Nancy Burke Best MA Thesis Award. The award is designed to promote outstanding MAs on Canadian topics written in Poland (in Polish, French or English), which contribute to a better understanding of Canada in Poland. The award is consistent with a wider strategy of fostering a new generation of Canadianists. The Association also contributes to the costs of lecture tours of invited guests among whom one can find Canadian Francophone and Anglophone literature professors, sociologists, film directors, writers, poets, and journalists. Moreover, the Association co-sponsors outreach programmes, like the Days of Canadian Culture organized by the Canadian Centre of the University of Silesia, and contributes significantly to the publications of books and articles on Canadian topics.

The publication of the first issue of *TransCanadiana* in 2008 was an important event for PACS. After the first five annual issues, in 2013 they started publishing their bulletin online. The latest issue, printing 35 essays and reviews, is devoted to the discussion of the impact of global conflicts on Canadian literature and society. Every issue (in Polish, English and

French) publishes about a dozen essays, several reviews, plus a list of
Nancy Burke Best MA Thesis Awards.

*****

In the closing part of this chapter I want to add just a few remarks
about Australian and New Zealand studies which are developing in Polish
universities and teacher training colleges in the last few years (including
South African and Postcolonial studies). The strongest centres are in
Opole, Toruń and Silesia, with the Universities in Poznań and Warsaw
also offering courses in literature, where students are encouraged to focus
on the work of Australian, New Zealand, South African and Postcolonial
writers. There were numerous MA papers, and more recently several
PhD dissertations (some of them published by Polish university presses
and others abroad, in Germany, the United Kingdom and India) on such
authors as Salman Rushdie, Patrick White, Peter Carey, David Malouf,
Thomas Keneally, Tim Winton, J.M. Coetzee and Helen Gardner. Among
African writers, Polish readers and students of literature seem to hold special respect for Nigerian writers: Wole Soyinka, Chinua Achebe, Ben Okri,
and more recently Chimamanda Ngozi Adichie, but naturally they are
also well acquainted with the work of South African Nobel prize winners,
Nadine Gordimer and J.M. Coetzee. English language Asian writers are
also attracting the attention of Polish scholars: it all started with the publication of Salman Rushdie's *Midnight's Children* in 1981 (Polish edition
1989), but the work of the younger generation of writers is also examined in conference papers, critical essays and dissertations. For instance,
I had the pleasure of supervising a Ph. D. thesis at Warsaw University
about the novels by Salman Rushdie, Vikram Seth and Amit Chaudhuri,
written by Patrycja Austin and published in India in 2014: *In Words and
Music: Global Imaginaries in the Novels of Rushdie, Seth and Chaudhuri.*
Professor Ryszard Wolny from Opole supervised two Ph. D. papers written
by young scholars there: Rachael Sumner's *Writing from the Margins of
Europe,* and Tomasz Gadzina's *Tim Winton: Narrating the Country and
Nation;* both books are published by Peter Lang in a series *Silesian Studies
in Anglophone Cultures and Literatures*, co-edited by Professor Wolny,
President of the Polish Association for Studies of Australasia (PASA). He
is also working on *A Short History of Australian Literature.*

Scholars from the University of Opole often host international conferences in Australian studies. The first one was called *Australia: Identity, Memory, Destiny,* and took place in 2006; recently they invited scholars from several countries to present papers on *Historical Heritage and Contemporary Perspectives in Language, Culture and Literature.* One of the aims of the conference was to establish and hold the first general meeting of the Polish Association for Studies of Australasia (PASA). The idea for the Association was inspired by a conference organized a year earlier, in 2016, by the Faculty of English at the Adam Mickiewicz University in Poznań, entitled *Europe and Down Under: Bridging Gaps and Fostering Connections.* The conference brought together Polish, German and Australian scholars of literary and cultural studies as well as history and linguistics. The interest in the conference prompted the organizers and participants to create an organization that would create a network of Polish and international scholars of the Australasian region. Today, the Polish Association is part of InASA (International Australian Studies Association). Its President is Professor Ryszard Wolny from Opole University: he published extensively on *Australian Poetry in the New Millennium,* on *Australian Modernist Theatre*, and on *Australian Literature of the Great War.* He supervised many MA and two PhD dissertations on Australian and Postcolonial literature and culture. Silesian University in Katowice has a very active Department of Postcolonial Studies, part of its Institute of English Cultures and Literatures. For October 2018 the University plans a cycle of events connected with their 50th anniversary, including the honorary doctorate which the University will confer on J.M. Coetzee.

Nicholas Copernicus University in Toruń offers a number of postgraduate courses in language, culture, literature and media of English-speaking countries outside Europe. One interesting example is a postgraduate course called *Australian Studies* devised by Doctor Waldemar Skrzypczak: there are lectures and seminars on a variety of subjects, but also discussions, film shows and workshops, including history before and after 1788, Aboriginal cultures and ethnic diversity, dominant literary themes in poetry, fiction and non-fiction writing. At Warsaw University, the literary review *Anglica* plans for autumn 2018 the publication of a collection of essays on Australian and New Zealand literature.

* * * * * *

Acknowledgements

I would like to acknowledge the help of my colleagues, Heads of English Departments and Institutes of English Studies in Poland who kindly provided me, during the academic year 2015/2016, with useful information about scholarly activities of their schools. The reports I received were detailed and exhaustive; I can only apologize for shortening them in the presentation prepared by me for the 2016 IAUPE Conference at University College London. Any omissions or oversights are entirely my own fault. Facts and figures in the second and third sections of this text are taken from PAAS (Polish Association for American Studies) and PACS (Polish Association for Canadian Studies) newsletters, published in the last twenty years or so. Special thanks are due to the following colleagues: Professor Małgorzata Grzegorzewska and Doctor Piotr Szymczak, Warsaw University; Professor Krystyna Stamirowska, Jagiellonian University in Kraków; Professor Katarzyna Dziubalska-Kołaczyk, Adam Mickiewicz University, Poznań; Professor Jean Ward and Professor Marek Wilczyński, Gdańsk University; Professor Ryszard Wolny, Opole University; Doctor Grzegorz Moroz and Doctor Jerzy Kamionowski, Białystok University; Doctor Agnieszka Kallaus, Reszów University; Ms Elżbieta Foltyńska, MA, Secretary of PASE (The Polish Association for the Study of English), Professor Tomasz Basiuk, President of PAAS (The Polish Association for American Studies), Professor Anna Branach-Kallas, President of PACS (The Polish Association for Canadian Studies), and Professor Ryszard Wolny, President of PASA (The Polish Association for Studies of Australasia).

Zdeněk Beran

English Literary Studies in the Czech Republic

Abstract: A new, vigorous impulse for English Literary Studies (ELS) in the Czech speaking territory came after the 1989 "Velvet Revolution," which ended the decades-long period of Communism in Czechoslovakia. Since that time ELS has developed rapidly to become one of the most prominent areas of academic research and other scholarly activities in the Czech Republic. The present chapter maps the history of this recent development, comparing it with the conditions in the preceding decades, especially with the situation at Czech universities after the suppression of the politically liberal "Prague Spring" of 1968. The early 1990 saw a radical reform of English departments at the three traditional Czech universities (Charles University in Prague, Masaryk University in Brno and Palacký University in Olomouc) and the first attempts to found new universities, which would also provide programmes including English Literary Studies. Due to this, ELS is also taught at seven regional and one private Czech universities in the present time. All these centres are active not only in teaching Anglophone literatures in their BA, MA and PhD courses, but also in participating in international projects, organizing international conferences and congresses, and publishing academic journals. Last but not least, Czech scholars play an indispensable role in popularizing Anglophone literatures as translators and authors of critical editions of the most representative texts such as Shakespeare's plays or English mediaeval poetry.

Keywords: English Literary Studies, Czech universities, Czech departments of English, conferences, academic journals, Czech translations of Anglophone literatures, Communism

The aim of this chapter is to map English Literary Studies at Czech universities during the last two and a half decades. The year 1990 is a turning point in its history, for obvious reasons: the Velvet Revolution, which took place in the last weeks of 1989, ended a long period of the Communist regime in Czechoslovakia and, in consequence, liberated the sphere of education (especially tertiary education) from the tyranny of restrictive ideology and strict political control. As a result, English Studies made rapid progress in the early 1990s, being supported by the British Council and other organizations and institutions. This enabled the English departments at the three existing Czech universities to grow in number both in terms of students and teachers, to transform into modern institutions and to launch ambitious projects and attractive teaching programmes. In addition, since that time new universities have been founded with English departments specializing both in linguistic and literary studies, new academic journals have appeared and such events as regularly held conferences and lectures given by prominent speakers have become a natural part of academic life.

To understand the significance of this change, a brief glimpse into the years preceding this development seems necessary. Before 1990, there were three universities in the Czech Republic (called then Czech Socialist Republic, as one of the two federal states of the Communist Czechoslovakia), whose faculties of Arts and Education provided instruction in English Studies, as part of the qualification of future primary or secondary school teachers. These universities were: Charles University in Prague, Jan Evangelista Purkyně University (today's Masaryk University) in Brno and Palacký University in Olomouc. The English Departments of their Faculties of Arts, especially, have a rich history, dating back to the early 20th century and boasting of significant experts both in English linguistics and in English and American literature. The Prague department, the oldest one, was founded in 1912 by Vilém Mathesius, since 1909 a Docent (Associate Professor) for "English language and literature" and later, since 1926, a key figure of the Prague Linguistic Circle. Mathesius taught both linguistic and literary courses. Other notable Prague experts in English and American literature include Otakar Vočadlo, Zdeněk Vančura, Zdeněk Stříbrný, Jaroslav Hornát, and Radoslav Nenadál. A critical moment for this department, as well as for the whole faculty and in fact for Czechoslovak humanities in general, came after 1970, when the new Communist leaders, installed after the Warsaw Pact invasion, started their relentless purges: first, several teachers were forced to leave the Department as being found disloyal to the new political system and to the consequent changes affecting both the faculty and university: O. Vočadlo, Z. Stříbrný and J. Hornát were not allowed to conduct their classes at Charles any more (Vočadlo retired, Stříbrný was offered a less significant position of a translator at the Faculty of Mathematics, Hornát could open courses in English drama at the School of Dramatic Arts);

in the mid-1970s another English literature expert and excellent translator of Anglophone literature, Jarmila Emmerová, was transferred to the Department of Translation Studies. Not only was the number of teachers and researchers reduced, but during the 1970s the Department also lost its independent status, as it was incorporated into the Department of Germanic Studies.[1] Contacts with the English-speaking countries, such as conference attendance or invited lecturers, were also drastically restricted. Moreover, some of the Department members were contacted by the secret police which intended to monitor, control and in effect destabilize the situation in the academic world of the 1970s and 1980s.[2] The Gorbachev era in the latter half of the 1980s, however, brought some hope. In 1987, it became possible for the English Department to emancipate itself from the Department of Germanic Studies and elect a new head, Martin Hilský, who was, moreover, not a member of the Communist Party. There were even modest attempts to enlarge the Department and attract new, young lecturers in the pre-Revolution months.

The other two universities were only slightly less affected by such strict political measures but their life did not resemble the desired academic freedom either. They had their own specific histories, though. Masaryk University in Brno was founded in 1919, within months following the creation of Czechoslovakia as a new post-war political formation. English Literary Studies became an organic part of its Faculty of Arts' programme at the very beginning, the greatest figure of the inter-bellum period being František Chudoba, a Shakespeare scholar, author of the two-volume *Kniha o Shakespearovi* (The Book of Shakespeare, 1941, 1943). During the Communist rule the Brno English Department achieved international prestige in linguistics rather than literary studies, with such world-renowned specialists as Josef Vachek, Jan Firbas and Josef Hladký.

The Olomouc English Department was founded in 1946 and its early history is connected especially with the name of Jiří Levý, founder of Czech Translation Studies. Levý died prematurely in 1967 and thus was

---

1 See Jakub Jareš, Matěj Spurný and Katka Volná, eds., *Náměstí Krasnoarmějců 2: Učitelé a studenti Filozofické fakulty v období normalizace* (Praha: Univerzita Karlova v Praze, 2012), p. 72.
2 See Jareš, Spurný and Volná, eds., *Náměstí Krasnoarmějců 2*, pp. 244, 262, 266.

not subject to the new academic policy of the early 1970s, when some English scholars were forced to leave (the linguists Macháček and Peprník) and the English Department had to fuse, just as the Prague one, with the German Department. Since 1972, however, the development of Olomouc literary studies was guided by Josef Jařab, who became a respected expert in American literature and whose personal integrity won him a position of the first post-revolution rector of Palacký University in 1990.

The contemporary situation of English Literary Studies at these three universities reflects the new role humanities began to play under the new political system. At Charles University, this discipline is pursued by the Department of Anglophone Literatures and Cultures of the Faculty of Arts, but also, in part, by the Department of Translation Studies of the same faculty, and by the English Department of the Faculty of Education. The Department of Anglophone Literatures and Cultures (DALC) was created in 2008, when the original Department of English and American Studies split into two separate but cooperating departments (offering a common BA programme), the other one being the Department of English Language and English Language Teaching (ELT) Methodology. The DALC provides BA, MA and PhD programmes in English Literary and Cultural Studies, participates actively in the Erasmus and TEAM international programmes, organizes conferences, and hosts renowned writers and scholars. Structurally, it is divided into two sections and three centres, the English Literature Section (directed by Martin Procházka, the former Head of Department), the American Literature and Cultural Studies Section (directed by Erik Roraback), the Centre for British and Commonwealth Studies (directed by Soňa Nováková), the Centre for Irish Studies (directed by Ondřej Pilný) and the Centre for Critical and Cultural Theory (directed by Louis Armand). Among these, especially the Centre for Irish Studies has achieved a significant position, receiving financial support from Irish governmental and cultural organizations. The Centre's most ambitious projects include an extended James Joyce research and a bibliography of Czech and Slovak translations from Irish literature together with reflections of Czech writers and intellectuals on Irish culture and politics. Due to the relentless effort of such Centre members as Ondřej Pilný, Clare Wallace, Louis Armand and Daniel Samek, the Centre manages to keep contacts with other research centres in Europe and to organize symposia and other events regularly. From the other prominent Department members of the recent years, it is necessary to mention the late Zdeněk Stříbrný, who returned to the Department in 1990, Martin Hilský, today a respected Shakespeare scholar and translator, and Martin Procházka, an expert in literary theory, English Romanticism and other fields of English and American Literary Studies.

The Department of Translation Studies focuses mostly on translations and other forms of Czech-English cultural exchange. Among its members, Stanislav Rubáš, the current Head of Department, researches in the field of translation mostly from English and Russian, while Šárka Tobrmanová is perhaps the only contemporary Czech expert on the works of John Milton and Eva Kalivodová combines her interests in the history of translation with research work in gender studies. Its former member, the recently deceased Jiří Josek, was another distinguished translator of Shakespeare's plays and poetry, as well as other works of English and American literature, both classical and modern. As has been said, the Department of English Language and Literature at the Faculty of Education in Prague participates actively in English Literary Studies too. This tradition has been revived mainly by the late Anna Grmelová, who came to Prague from the Slovak University of Prešov, after the split of Czechoslovakia in the early 1990s, and whose contribution to the study of English Modernism, and especially the work of D. H. Lawrence, is indisputable. Nowadays, the studies are pursued by the current Department head Petr Chalupský, who specializes in the contemporary English novel, and Jakub Ženíšek, whose field is American literature.

The Department of English and American Studies of Masaryk University has also developed into one of the largest departments of its Faculty of Arts. The only current full-time Professor of the Department, Milada Franková, has published extensively on contemporary British women writers, beginning with her 1995 monograph on Iris Murdoch. M. M. Kaylor has contributed significantly to the study of English gay culture, as reflected in 19th century English fiction and poetry. Tomáš Pospíšil is director of one of the two special sections of the Department, the Centre for North-American Studies, and his major field of interest covers American film, TV and other media.

Similarly, the Olomouc Department of English and American Studies received an invigorating stimulus for its development in the early 1990s. Nowadays its major focus seems to be on American Studies, especially due to the research concerns of the two of Jařab's disciples, Marcel Arbeit and Michal Peprník (son of the linguist Jaroslav Peprník). The conferences organized at Olomouc are oriented predominantly towards US literature and media, and its academic publications, both journals and books, tend to address topics related to American culture too. But as the Olomouc Department is perhaps the largest one in the Czech Republic, with its thirty-five teachers, they are able to provide various other courses and launch other projects, such as modern poetry translation or Augustan satire.

Contemporary English Literary Studies in the Czech Republic can hardly be imagined without activities of the new-founded regional universities with their English departments. The rise of these institutions testifies to the fact that there has been a growing need for tertiary education in humanities since 1990. One of the first was Ostrava University, opened in October 1991, having been transformed from the local Faculty of Education. The Department of English and American Studies was established in the following year. One of its founding fathers, Stanislav Kolář, has become an expert in American Jewish literature, while other Department members research in contemporary Afro-American female fiction or American popular culture.

The University of Hradec Králové keeps its Department of English Language and Literature at the Faculty of Education, transformed from the original regional faculty of Charles University in the early 1990s. The key figure in its English Literary Studies is Bohuslav Mánek, an expert in the history of Czech translations and publications of English poetry and fiction. Otherwise this department does not specialize in literary studies, its focus being prevailingly the English Language and ELT Methodology. Situated not far from Hradec, the University of Pardubice received its current status in 1994; in 2000 the Faculty of Humanities became part of its structure and in 2005 it was renamed to the Faculty of Arts. The Department of English and American Studies has existed since the 1990s, first specializing in ELT Methodology, but at present time offering a much more variegated programme, including English and American Culture Studies. Šárka Bubíková publishes on American ethnic literature, Olga Roebuck's concern is Scottish literature and Ladislav Vít writes on the poetics of place, especially in modern poetry. Another important centre of English Literary Studies is the University of South Bohemia in České

Budějovice, with two Departments of English Studies, one at the Faculty of Arts, founded in 2010, the other at the Faculty of Education, founded in 1988. Of these, the younger one is developing rapidly and vigorously, directed by Ladislav Nagy, an expert in contemporary British fiction and especially the historical novel. At another regional university, the University of West Bohemia in Pilsen, the programme of English Literary Studies is represented by Justin Quinn, a poet and novelist and, most of all, respected expert in American and Irish poetry. Jan Evangelista Purkyně University in Ústí nad Labem (North Bohemia) received its full status in 1991. Its Department of English is part of the Faculty of Education, and as such, it organizes its teaching programme mostly around ELT courses; its literature classes, however, are conducted by Colin Clark, perhaps our best expert in contemporary Scottish literature. Tomáš Baťa University in Zlín, founded in 2003, opened its Faculty of Humanities in 2007. Though the purpose of this institution has been defined primarily with the view of teaching foreign languages for technical professions, its Department of Modern Languages and Literatures is very active in organizing other events too, including annual conferences hosting speakers from all over the world.

Apart from the above mentioned public universities, English Literary Studies are also pursued at a private institution, the Metropolitan University in Prague (MUP), founded in 2008. Its Department of English Studies not only offers BA and MA courses in English and American Literature, which are part of its English Studies programme, but organizes conferences of its own, welcoming students' participation in these events, and encourages contacts with other universities worldwide. Though the MUP focuses mainly on political sciences, international relations and history, English Studies makes an indispensable part of their programme. The *spiritus agens* of its literature courses is Klára Kolinská, an expert in Canadian literature, and some courses are also taught by Charles University teachers, such as Martin Procházka, Ondřej Pilný and myself.

As has been mentioned, most of these departments organize conferences and publish their own periodicals. Perhaps the greatest event in this respect was the Ninth World Shakespeare Congress, held in Prague on 17–22 July, 2011. The congress was initiated by Zdeněk Stříbrný and organized jointly by Charles University and the National Theatre.

It hosted about 600 participants and its keynote speakers were Stanley Wells, Marjorie Garber, Djanet Sears and Martin Hilský. The seminar sessions and workshops were held in the main Faculty of Arts building, but the keynote speeches and performances took place in two major Prague theatres, the National Theatre and the Estate Theatre, where also the plenary on "Directing Shakespeare: The Cold War Years" was held. The congress was accompanied by other events, such as visits to several historical places outside Prague, though Prague itself offered a lot of opportunities for the participants to get culturally satiated.

This was an event of utmost significance, indeed. Nevertheless, there are many further conferences organized on a regular basis throughout the Czech Republic. Thus the Prague Centre for Irish Studies held a series of colloquia on the work of James Joyce in 2003, 2005 and 2007, a colloquium on Beckett in 2006 and two major conferences, the 2010 International James Joyce Symposium and the 2005 annual conference of the International Association for the Study of Irish Literatures. Another notable conference organized by the Department of Anglophone Literatures and Cultures in Prague during recent years was the 15th International Conference of the Utopian Studies Society ("Utopia and Nonviolence"), held in July 2014.

Nevertheless, the longest tradition in conference organizing should be granted to the Masaryk University Department, whose Brno International Conference in English, American and Canadian Studies saw its tenth session in 2015, running continuously albeit irregularly since 1986, i.e. for more than three decades. During that time it has developed into one of the most popular events for English scholars not only from the Czech Republic but also from abroad, as Brno provides a pleasant and friendly venue for such meetings.

The Olomouc Department has organized The International Colloquium of American Studies mostly on annual basis since the mid-1990s. These colloquia cover various attractive topics such as "Spirituality and Religion in American Culture," "(Mis)understanding Postmodernism" or "Assimilation in America: A Good or a Bad Word?" This is another long-going tradition as the year 2017 saw its 21st session. The Zlín University organized its 8th annual English Studies conference entitled "From Theory to Practice" in September 2016. Occasionally, conferences addressing English Literary Studies issues are held to cover specific topics or to discuss the work of outstanding persons, both Czech and English. Thus the Metropolitan University in Prague organized a conference on "Czech Receptions of 'Other Literatures in English'" in early 2016, or the Department of Translation Studies at Charles University commemorated the significant translator of English fiction and poetry, Jan Zábrana, at a conference held in autumn 2015. In 2016, a similar session was dedicated to the Charlotte Brontë bicentenary, an event hosted by the Department of Philosophy at Charles, with contributions from scholars as well as students.

Publications are an integral part of all this work and many English departments in the Czech Republic publish their own academic journals, which provide a large forum for scholars as well as PhD students. Some periodicals have survived the fall of Communism and continue to come out in a new format, with modern layouts and different editorial policies, keeping the high standard of their first issues. *Prague Studies in English* is such a traditional journal, incorporated in the larger series of Acta Universitatis Carolinae, published by the Faculty of Arts, Charles University in Prague. Though issued irregularly, it gives equal space to its linguistic and literary sections. The Department of Anglophone Literatures and Cultures publishes *Litteraria Pragensia*, the journal which emerged in 1991 when its predecessor, *Philologica Pragensia*, split into two separate periodicals (the other being *Linguistica Pragensia*). In the first years it accepted contributions from different national literatures but soon it specialized in English and American writings and accepted articles written in English only. Today its numbers, usually three at a year, are organized thematically and carefully edited by appointed editors. Since 2002 a series of Litteraria Pragensia Books has been issued alongside, providing an opportunity for English scholars to publish their monographs or essay collections.

Brno Studies in English can boast a similar long tradition, being founded in 1959 by Josef Vachek and now entering the sixth decade of its existence. Like the previous two, it is a peer-reviewed academic journal, publishing articles in both English linguistics and literary studies. In 2009 it became an independent publication (no more part of the Brno Faculty of Arts Series) and since then two numbers have been issued each year. New academic journals include the *Moravian Journal of Literature and Film*, first appearing in autumn 2009 and bringing out two numbers annually since then. This peer-reviewed journal is prepared by its editor-in-chief Marcel Arbeit of Palacký University and managing editor Roman Trušník of Tomáš Baťa University in Zlín. The *Ostrava Journal of English Philology*, founded in the same year, is defined as "a bi-annual peer-reviewed scholarly journal … that provides a space for original research articles in the field of linguistics and literary/cultural studies related to English-speaking countries." More than other journals it invites papers written by PhD students, whose research may, in this way, receive a very useful feedback. In Eastern Bohemia two academic journals thrive: the *Hradec Králové Journal of Anglophone Studies*, another peer-reviewed academic magazine, saw its fourth volume in 2017 under the editorship of Michaela Marková, while the Pardubice editorial team is preparing the ninth volume of their own peer-reviewed *American and British Studies Annual*, published by Pavel Mervart Publishing. Among the periodical publications of the Czech Faculties of Education, the *Prague Journal of English Studies*, with its six completed volumes, has become an arena for both Czech and international scholars' essays in linguistics and literary studies.

The last part of this overview will be dedicated to the most important book publications of the Czech scholars in the field of English Literary Studies. Martin Hilský has devoted the last thirty years of his career to a single, overriding task, to present a modern Czech version of the complete works of William Shakespeare. This ambitious project was completed in 2012 with immense success. After a series of commented bilingual editions of several individual plays and sonnets, that year saw a one-volume mammoth edition of the complete Shakespeare in Czech, a genuine Shakespeare/Hilský folio. The project is the more important since Shakespeare's entire dramatic and poetic work has never before been translated into Czech by a single translator. The edition was received with a very high acclaim and the publisher has promptly prepared a new, extended version for 2016. Two years earlier Hilský published a huge volume titled *Shakespeare a jeviště svět* (Shakespeare and the Stage of the World), comprising his critical interpretations of Shakespeare's dramas. These two books added fundamentally to the long line of Czech Shakespearean publications, which also include Zdeněk Stříbrný's *Shakespeare and Eastern Europe* (2000) and *The Whirligig of Time: Essays on Shakespeare and Czechoslovakia* (2006), and Jiří Josek's bilingual edition of his translation of Shakespeare's plays and poems, including more than thirty volumes. Another noteworthy achievement in Czech reception of English culture was the first complete translation and critical edition of *Beowulf* (2003), prepared by Jan Čermák, a first rate expert in Anglo-Saxon culture, from the Department of English Language and ELT Methodology, Charles University. Martin Procházka published his *Romantismus a romantismy* (Romanticism and Romanticisms), a monograph on the European Romantic movement, written jointly with Zdeněk Hrbata, in 2006. Besides, his recent English publications include *Transversals* (2007) and *Ruins in the New World* (2012). One of the most prolific academicians of the Prague Department is Louis Armand, whose books rank from poetry and fiction to academic writings such as *Techne: James Joyce, Hypertext and Technology* (2003), *Solicitations: Essays on Criticism and Culture* (2005), *Incendiary Devices: Discourses of the Other* (2006), *Literate Technologies: Language, Cognition, Technicity* (2006), *Event States: Discourse, Time, Mediality* (2007), *The Organ-Grinder's Monkey* (2013), and *Videology* (2015). Ondřej Pilný researches mostly in modern Irish and English drama, in *Irony and Identity in Modern Irish Drama* (2006) and *The Grotesque in Contemporary Anglophone Drama* (2016), while his colleague Clare Wallace contributed to the same area with her *Suspect Cultures: Narrative, Identity and Citation in 1990s New Drama* (2006) and *The Theatre of David Greig* (2013). Among other publications of Prague English Literary Studies, a dictionary of English writers (*Slovník spisovatelů: Anglie etc.* 1996, 2003) should not be ignored, as it was the first project around which the Department grouped after the Velvet Revolution of 1989.

The Brno scholar Milada Franková's most noteworthy publications include *Human Relationships in the Novels of Iris Murdoch* (1995), *Britské spisovatelky na konci tisíciletí* (British Women Writers at the End of the Millennium, 1999), and *Britské spisovatelky na přelomu tisíciletí* (British Women Writers at the Turn of the Millennium, 2003), while Micheal Kaylor of the same Department brought his ground-breaking study *Secreted Desires: The Major Uranians: Hopkins, Pater and Wilde* in 2006 and a two-volume anthology of gay literature, *Lad's Love*, in 2010. Tomáš Pospíšil published his monograph *The Progressive Era in American Historical Fiction: John Dos Passos's* 42nd Parallel *and E. L. Doctorow's* Ragtime in 1998 and eleven years later he co-authored *Us-Them-Me: the*

Search for Identity in Canadian Literature and Film. Michal Peprník of the Olomouc department contributed to topological studies with his *Topos lesa v americké literatuře* (The Topos of the Forest in American Literature, 2005) and with the first volume of his intended large J. F. Cooper monograph in 2011. Marcel Arbeit's (of the same Department) monumental publication is the three-volume *Bibliografie americké literatury v českých překladech ... do r. 1997* (Bibliography of American Literature in Czech Translation ... Up To 1997, 2000), comprising entries of book publications, supplemented by an electronic database of magazine publications of the examined period. In 2016, Ladislav Nagy published his book-length study *Palimpsesty, heterotopie a krajiny: Historie v anglickém románu posledních desetiletí* (Palimpsests, Heterotopiae and Landscapes: History in the English Novel of the Last Decades) and Petr Poslední of Pardubice University came with an inspiring collection of essays *Jiný Conrad: eseje o literární kultuře* (Another Conrad: Essays in Literary Culture), in which he confronts the English writer with other, mostly non-English, novelists and storytellers. Justin Quinn's criticism has been collected in several volumes, including *Gathered Beneath the Storm: Wallace Stevens, Nature and Community* (2002), *American Errancy: Empire, Sublimity and Modern Poetry* (2005), *The Cambridge Introduction to Modern Irish Poetry, 1800–2000* (2008) and *Between Two Fires: Transnationalism and Cold War Poetry* (2015).

Many more books and other publications of various kind could be mentioned as well; their line seems almost endless. Some of the above mentioned scholars are also excellent translators, and translation can obviously be regarded as a specific form of enrichment of English Literary Studies. The field is fruitful and the harvest is more and more abundant each year. And this is exactly of what we had dreamt about thirty years ago – luckily, nowadays we can conclude with a great deal of confidence that our dreams have come true.

Bibliography

Havránek, Jan and Zdeněk Pousta, eds. *Dějiny Univerzity Karlovy* IV. 1918–1990, Prague: Karolinum, 1998.

Jareš, Jakub, Matěj Spurný and Katka Volná, eds. *Náměstí Krasnoarmějců 2: Učitelé a studenti Filozofické fakulty v období normalizace*, Prague: Univerzita Karlova v Praze, 2012.

Department websites

Department of Anglophone Literatures and Cultures, Faculty of Arts, Charles University, Prague: http://ualk.ff.cuni.cz

Department of Anglophone Studies, Metropolitan University, Prague: http://www.mup.cz/en/about-mup/mup-departments/department-of-anglophone-studies

Department of English, Faculty of Arts, University of South Bohemia, České Budějovice: http://www.ff.jcu.cz/ustav-anglistiky

Department of English, Faculty of Education, Jan Evangelista Purkyně University, Ústí nad Labem: https://www.pf.ujep.cz/kaj

Department of English and American Studies, Faculty of Arts, Masaryk University, Brno: http://www.phil.muni.cz/wkaa

Department of English and American Studies, Faculty of Arts, Ostrava University: http://ff.osu.cz/kaa

Department of English and American Studies, Faculty of Arts, Palacký University, Olomouc: http://www.anglistika.upol.cz

Department of English and American Studies, Faculty of Arts, Pardubice University: https://ff.upce.cz/ff/kaa.html

Department of English Language and Literature, Faculty of Education, Charles University, Prague: http://webkajl.pedf.cuni.cz

Department of English Language and Literature, Faculty of Education, University of Hradec Králové: https://www.uhk.cz/cs-CZ/PDF/Katedry/Katedra-anglickeho-jazyka-a-literatury-(1)#UHK-Article

Department of English Language and Literature, Faculty of Arts, University of West Bohemia, Plzeň: https://kaj.zcu.cz

Department of Modern Languages and Literatures, Faculty of Humanities, Tomáš Baťa University, Zlín: http://www.utb.cz/fhs-en/structure/about-us-1

Department of Translation Studies, Faculty of Arts, Charles University, Prague: http://utrl.ff.cuni.cz

Olha Bandrovska

Literature of Great Britain and the United States of America in Contemporary Ukrainian Literary Studies: Scholarly Accomplishments and Pain Points

Abstract: The article examines current institutional forms and scholarly trends of English and American studies in Ukraine. The conception of teaching and studying Anglophone literature inherited from the Soviet university model is aimed to comprehend literature of English-speaking countries in comparison with other European literary traditions and in the relevant historical and cultural contexts. It is argued that despite the complexities and contradictions of societal and mental changes during recent decades, Ukrainian scholars have remained committed to researching the most fundamental and topical issues concerning the study of Anglophone literature, as well as to spiritual re-orientation of Ukrainian nation towards the open non-corrupt society and democratic freedoms.

Keywords: Ukraine, English studies, American studies, Anglophone literature, world literature, Ukraine's top universities, philological education

The beginnings of English studies in Ukraine date back to the late 19th and early 20th centuries when Ukrainian writers Mykhailo Starytsky, Panteleimon Kulish, and Ivan Franko, among others, translated a number of the most prominent works of English literature into the Ukrainian language. The works they initially translated include those by Shakespeare, John Milton, Lord Byron, and Percy Bysshe Shelley. Starytsky, Kulish, and Franko were conscious of the huge significance the translations would bear in helping Ukrainians master the highest achievements of world literature and culture. Fairly sharp debates about the accomplishments and flaws of these first English-Ukrainian translations also accelerated the emergence of Ukrainian literary studies and have resulted in far-reaching consequences: First, they laid the foundation for academic studies in the theory and practice of translation during the 20th century, and second, they contributed to strengthening the enterprise of literary criticism. For instance, Franko is called the founder of Ukrainian Shakespearian studies since his translations, editing activity, prefaces, and essays on Shakespeare's works have remained relevant up to today.

During the Soviet period (1922–91), Ukrainian English studies received institutional anchoring. In 1926, the Shevchenko Institute of Literature was founded as a structural subdivision of the National Academy of Sciences of Ukraine. The main direction of its activity was intensive research on Ukrainian and world literature. Preparing fundamental theoretical, historical, and literary studies; textbooks, schoolbooks, encyclopedias, and reference books was the task of the newly created Department of Foreign Literature. However, the department's main focus was to study Western European and American literature.

From the 1930s to the '60s, departments of world literature were established in leading Ukrainian universities in Kyiv, Lviv, Dnipropetrovs'k,[1] Chernivtsi, and other cities. It is noteworthy that Anglistics, which historically concerned itself with the study of the languages, cultures, and literature of English-speaking countries, was divided into two independent structural units. The English language component complemented by geographical, historical, and cultural aspects was taught by the departments of English philology, while English and American literature comprised part of lecture courses covering the history of world literature and were delivered by the world literature departments. The course content was mainly oriented towards studying Western European literature and literature from the United States of America. The advantage of this approach to the organization of philological education was that it made it possible to comprehend English literature in comparison with other European literary traditions and in the relevant historical and cultural contexts of a particular era. The basis of the Soviet model of studying foreign literature came from Goethe, who argued that "National literature is now rather an unmeaning term; the epoch of world-literature is at hand, and everyone must strive to hasten its approach."[2] This model, aimed at studying the

---

1   The official name of the city was changed to Dnipro in 2016.
2   *Conversations of Goethe with Eckermann and Soret*, trans. by John Oxenford (London: Smith, Elder & Co, 1850), Vol. I, p. 351.

mutual influence of national literatures and cultures, is preserved in modern Ukrainian literary studies.

The biggest disadvantage of the Soviet educational system was the communist ideology indoctrination that permeated all phases of instruction. Hence, world literature as an academic discipline had also been under its ideological pressure; therefore, ideological rather than aesthetic factors were often decisive in deeming which authors would be the focus for lecture courses as well as critical analysis. For instance, modernist and avant-garde literature of the 20th century was declared a bourgeois art that cultivated decadent moods, whereas writers such as Jack London or Theodore Dreiser who illustrated the principles of class division and struggle were rated much higher. Only in the late 1980s, the period of democratization of the Soviet Union (known as *perestroika*), quite a lot of British and American authors (the most revealing name is George Orwell) were introduced to students and translated for readers. Furthermore, the ideological orientation of the humanities influenced the objects of scholarly investigation and the methods of academic literary criticism. As is stated in the *Great Soviet Encyclopedia*, "Soviet study of literary theory and criticism, which has developed in close connection with the cultural inquiries of the new society, thoroughly investigates literature, the origin and social implications of literature, the principles of the historical literary process, and the methods of artistic expression."[3] Despite the considerable influence of the sociological approach, especially of Marxism in Soviet literary criticism, the genealogy of Soviet literary criticism includes influential approaches and theories such as formalism and Mikhail Bakhtin's theories concerning the novel, genres, and the dialogic nature of literature.

The year Ukraine proclaimed its independence, 1991, is the starting point for the contemporary period of Ukrainian literary studies. The system of knowledge and education then began operating in new geopolitical, economic, and ideological contexts. Absolutely novel realities were marked by a crisis of cultural values that had been shaped and inculcated in people over the course of generations. As rightly observed by Solomiya Pavlychko (1958–99), an outstanding specialist in British and American

---

3 "Philological Education in the USSR," in: *The Great Soviet Encyclopedia*, 3rd ed., 1970–79, (Gale Group, Inc., 2010).

literature, at the end of the first decade of independence, Ukraine was a typical postcolonial society: "Its cultural discourse repeats the Soviet formulas and does not want to distance itself from 'classical' writers and ideas inherited from the past. At the same time, today's rethinking of cultural values and the modernization of cultural discourses is an urgent task."[4]

The same applies to the sphere of the humanities. Specialists in world literature, who due to their professional interests had always conveyed a more open, nonconformist view of world culture, understood better than most the complexities of restructuring and redefining Ukraine's national identity as well as the need to integrate Ukraine into European society. In 1999, when Ihab Hassan, Vilas professor emeritus, addressed the First International Conference on American Literature in Kyiv, he suggested that "What has become of postmodernism is geopolitical postmodernity: localism and globalism in struggle everywhere, margins and centres, minorities and majorities in struggle—but also the conflict of margins and margins, minorities and minorities, fragments and fragments. On how we resolve or reconcile or simply mediate these various conflicts, depends our future in Kiev, Innsbruck, Dhaka, and Milwaukee. But this reconciliation, this mediation will not succeed without some spiritual re-orientation."[5]

It is indicative that Hassan managed to generalize the most important mission for post-Soviet intelligentsia, for "spiritual re-orientation" has become the target that must have been achieved by Ukrainians. Thus, while preserving the best achievements of the previous period, an effective reformation of science and education became both the goal of the Ukrainian state and its academics.

In the years 2000–2016, Ukraine experienced two series of protests: the Orange Revolution of 2004 and the Euromaidan of 2014. These were powerful ideological confrontations in civil society and showed the struggle for economic survival. The general trend over recent years has

---

4   Соломія Павличко. "Насильство як метафора (Дискурс насильства в українсь кій літературі)," in: Павличко, Соломія. *Теорія літератури*, (Київ: Видавництв во Соломії Павличко "Основи", 2002). https//lit.wikireading.ru/37080.

5   Ihab Hassan. "What Was Postmodernism and What Will It Become?," in: *20th Century American Literature after Midcentury. International Conference Proceedings*, ed. Tamara Denysova, (Kyiv, 2000), p. 18.

had a variety of consequences on Ukrainian universities. The most important of these has been the positive reform of the higher educational system
that resulted in the adoption of the Bologna Process, and on the negative
side, there have been economic woes for the universities. Despite all the
difficulties, one could state that literary studies have been preserved and
are still being developing. Anglophone literature has been in the spotlight
of literary research in Ukraine's top universities and institutions.

The Shevchenko Institute of Literature as a part of the National
Academy of Sciences of Ukraine plays a central, coordinating role in the
area of literary studies in the country. The World Literature Department
was founded within the institute in 1962 and launched an extensive
research program on Western European literature. Under the administra-
tion of Professor Dmytro Zatonsky, the first head of the unit who later
was appointed as the director of the institute, English, American, and
Canadian literature were all established as fields of study.

It is no exaggeration to claim that Professor Tamara Denysova (1934–
2015), who is considered one of the most distinguished Soviet specialists
in American studies, was the founder of American studies in independent Ukraine. She wrote eight books of literary criticism, including *The
American Novels and Novelists of the 20th century* (1990) and *The
History of the Twentieth Century American Literature* (2002, 2012). In
addition to her outstanding personal contributions to literary criticism,
there is general agreement that she was the leading organizer of literary
studies in Anglophone literature.

In 2005, Denysova founded the Center for American Literary Studies
in Ukraine (CALSU) at the Shevchenko Institute of Literature. With the
support of the Public Affairs section of the US Embassy in Ukraine, this
professional voluntary association united experts in American literature from all regions of Ukraine. To date, CALSU has regional repre-
sentatives in more than twenty Ukrainian cities and towns. Its activities
include organizing conferences, symposiums, and seminars; editing the
CALSU yearbook, *American Literary Studies in Ukraine*; developing
and publishing different curricula on the subject; planning out courses
in American literature; and delivering academic and general lectures for
various audiences.

Special attention should be paid to the informal school that Denysova organized for the study of the history of American literature within CALSU. The first topics for relevant seminars were related to contemporary US literature, specifically postmodernism and multiculturalism. Later, colonial Puritan literature, the Enlightenment, romanticism, naturalism, and modernism were consistently propounded for discussion. The result of a year-long discussion of each period in the history of American literature was a symposium. From 1999 to 2016, two proceedings of international conferences on American literature (2000, 2004) were published, as well as nine issues of the journal *American Literary Studies in Ukraine*.

Canadian Studies in the institute has been represented by Professor Nataliya Ovcharenko, the head of the World Literature Department, who has edited four monographs on Canadian literature, including *Canadian Literary Canons at the Turn of the Century* (2006) and *Paradigm of Memory: Canadian Discourse: A Portrait of Timothy Irving Frederick Findley* (2011).

The traditions of the Kyiv Philological School for the study of world literature were formed throughout the 20th century in the Department of Foreign Literature (its historical name was the Department of Western European Literature) at Taras Shevchenko National University in Kyiv. From the time of its founding, Anglophone literature has been a major area of investigation. In particular, Professor Sergiy Rodzevych, one of the founders of Ukrainian Shakespearian studies, worked there in the 1930s. The model parameters that laid the foundation of the department's teaching school were aimed at creating a systematic, diversified, and high-quality study experience and encouraging the modern reception of world literature. From the 1960s to the '80s, Professor Tetyana Yakymovych, whose research interests focused on French literature of the 19th and 20th centuries, and Honoured Professor of Kyiv National University Kira Shakhova, the first Ukrainian specialist in Hungarian literature, organized an extensive program for the preparation of textbooks and manuals on Western European literature with special interest paid to English and American literature. In the 1980s and early '90s, further development of literary studies at the department was greatly influenced by Professor Dmytro Nalyvaiko, now a corresponding member of the National Academy of Sciences of Ukraine. Nalyvaiko made a significant contribution to the revision of the department's curriculum for historical literary and theoretical courses and helped restructure the concept of studying foreign literature during Ukraine's first years of independence.

In the years 1993–2003, for the first time in its history, the Department of Foreign Literature was chaired by a specialist in English studies, Professor Nataliya Zhluktenko. A recognized authority in modern British literature, she is the author of two scholarly monographs, numerous articles, prefaces to Ukrainian translations of English writers, and the co-author of the textbooks *The Issues of the Newest American Literature* (1981) and *English Literature: The Twentieth Century* (1987, 1993). The focal point of her research has been genre poetics of the 20th century novel, Shakespeare, the history and theory of literary criticism, and ecocriticism. Zhluktenko's monograph *English Psychological Novel of the 20th Century* (1988) on the psychological analysis of the characters' personality, ways of expressing the author's position, and the compositional and stylistic features of this genre in the works of Joseph Conrad, Arnold Bennett, Virginia Woolf, D. H. Lawrence, Iris Murdoch, John Fowles, and other English writers still remains a model of scholarly objectivity and depth. Meanwhile, her work on the implementation of a new concept for teaching and research in world literature has assumed even greater importance. In the first decade of independent Ukraine, joint scholarly symposiums hosted by the Department of Foreign Literature and the Shevchenko Institute of Literature have regularly taken place; Denysova, the leading Ukrainian researcher in American Studies, was invited to lecture, and Fulbright scholars from the United States taught in the department. This was the period during which the number of PhD theses on English literature defended at the department substantially increased.

In the years 2003–2013, the Department of Foreign Literature was chaired by Professor Sergiy Prigodiy (1953–2013), a specialist in American-Ukrainian comparative studies. He went on to create innovative programs and courses for specialization in Anglophone literature. Based on Prigodiy's initiative, the department has focused on topical literary approaches and methodologies in teaching the history of foreign literature. His personal achievement in this area concerns the introduction of the policriticism of American literature through the application of methodologies such as psychoanalysis, archetypal criticism, deconstruction, neo-historicism, and reader-response criticism.

Within the context of intensifying of American studies at the Department of Foreign Literature, the scholarly activity of Tetyana Myched deserves special attention. She joined the department in 2010 and from the start has been actively elaborating the special courses offered in American Literature. Her numerous publications, in particular, her textbook on the American Renaissance, are related to the Puritan tradition that she claims has shaped 19th century American literature in many different ways.

Today the specialists on English and American Literature, namely, Professors Zhluktenko and Myched and Associate Professors Lilia Miroshnychenko, Olha Boinitska, Nataliya Bilyk, and Nataliya Lubarets make up the core of the department of Foreign Literature at Taras Shevchenko National University.

A notable contribution to the study of British and American literature has been made by the Department of Theory and History of World Literature named after Professor Valentyna Fesenko at Kyiv National Linguistic University (the successor of the Kyiv State Pedagogical Institute of Foreign Languages). The department does not have a long history, though it is important that its establishment in 1996 fostered the movement to qualify the institution with the status of a university, and later of a national university, since the department provided the full cycle of philological disciplines, including the history of foreign literature, the theory of literature, and methods of teaching foreign literature.

Professor Nataliya Vysotska played a significant role in this process, and her research interests encompass contemporary US literature with a special focus on multi/trans-culturalism, ethnic literature, the drama and theatre of the United States, African-American Literature, and Shakespearian intertext in contemporary American drama. She is the author of the following monographs: *At the Crossroads of Civilizations: African-American Drama as a Multicultural Phenomenon* (1997), *The Unity of the Plural: Late 20th – early 21st Century American Literature in the Context of Cultural Pluralism* (2010), and *The Concept of Multiculturalism as a Factor in US Recent Literary History* (2012). Of particular note are her special courses "Contemporary Drama of the USA," "The Multicultural Dimension of US Literature," and "From the Saint to the Superman: US

National Cultural Mythology in Historical Perspective" that are taught with relevant textbooks. Vysotska actively provides international activity. She is the current president of the Fulbright Society in Ukraine, a member of the European Association for African-American Studies, and collaborates with the Russian Society for American Culture Studies. As a visiting professor, she has repeatedly given lectures in the United States, in particular, at California State University, Sacramento. Being a scholar of wide experience, Vysotska, who chaired the department in 2012–2016 and at present is the deputy head of the Center for American Literary Studies in Ukraine, directs her intellectual energy towards inspiring the younger generation of Anglophone literature researchers.

One of the most well-known and authoritative groups among Ukrainian scholarly communities is the school of Anglophone literature researchers at Oles Honchar Dnipro National University. For more than half a century, its World Literature Department has been a centre of study for the historical typology of national literature from the era of the Renaissance to the 20th century. The origins of this school come from the scholarly and pedagogical activities of Nina Schreider (1909–76). A graduate of the State Academy of Arts, a part of the Leningrad School of Russian formalism, Schreider was a student of various, sometimes opposing, scholarly schools of great philologists (Viktor Zhirmunsky, Stefan Mokulsky, Boris Eichenbaum, Ivan Sollertinsky, and Lev Scherba). She combined in her research the best traditions of classical and experimental literary studies of the 1920s and '30s. The research methodology, correlating the formalists' observation of the nature of a text to its classical historical, cultural, and literary background, that transforms and responds to the calls of time and scholarly discourse is still a part of the legacy of literary studies at the department. Schreider, a researcher of French romantic literature, became the true scientific leader of many scholars who chose to study the history of English literature, including Professors Alexander Belsky, Liudmyla Skuratovska, and Tetyana Potnitseva.

During the years 1968–84, under the chairmanship of Professor Lidiya Potemkina, the substantive capacity of Anglicists addressed the genesis, history, typology, and poetics of English prose from the Elizabethan period and in modern times. For the first time in Ukrainian philology, the works of Sir Philip Sydney, Thomas Nashe, Thomas Deloney, George Gascoigne,

Thomas Lodge, and Aphra Behn in their due contexts of the Renaissance, mannerism, and baroque were elaborated in detail.

A significant part of research in the field of English studies within the Dnipropetrovs'k Philological School is associated with the scientific work of Professor Skuratovska. She is among the first in the nation's literary criticism to have studied English romanticism (the poetry of William Blake, William Wordsworth, and Shelley), Charles Dickens's novels, children's literature in regard to its connection with fantasy literature and the classics of the 19th and early 20th centuries (Edward Lear, Lewis Carroll, Sebastian Barry, Charles Kingsley, Rudyard Kipling, and R. L. Stevenson), and modernism (Gerard Manley Hopkins, James Joyce, Woolf, and T. S. Eliot).

The highest standards of excellence in the spheres of scholarly, institutional, and conference activities were preserved and developed when in 1994 the department was headed by Professor Tetyana Potnitseva, one of the most recognized specialists in Anglo-American studies in Ukraine. She has published extensively on the topic of 19th century English literature with special interest paid to romanticism. American Studies at the department has also been represented by Potnitseva and her PhD students (US literature at the end of the 19th century and in postmodern times). Being a member of the International Association of University Professors of English, she actively takes part in the international conferences abroad.

At the present time, the scientific interests of specialists from the World Literature Department in English and American studies cover research on Elizabethan literature (Lidiya Privalova and Nataliya Vlasenko), the 18th century English novel (Svitlana Vatchenko and Olena Maksyutenko), classical literature of the 19th century (Skuratovska and Potnitseva), modernism (Skuratovska and Ella Honcharenko), postmodern and after-postmodern British and American literature (Potnitseva, Nataliya Veligina, and Oleksii Levchenko), and present-day English and American Literature in a comparative dimension (Victoria Lipina).

One of the leading centres of contemporary English studies in Eastern Ukraine is the city of Zaporizhzhya. Without exaggeration, much of the credit for this goes to Professor Nataliya Torkut, who comes from Dnipropetrovs'k Philological School and is known for her work on a broad range of issues relevant to the English Renaissance, in particular, on the genesis, poetics, and genre system of English prose from the late Renaissance. The author of numerous articles on Shakespeare, Torkut is closely involved in the work of the European Shakespeare Research Association and the International Shakespeare Center (Timişoara, Romania). However, the most substantial contribution to Ukrainian Anglistics concerns her initiatives in organizing scholarly activities in Ukraine and popularizing Shakespearian literary works among Ukrainian readers. In 1998, under her leadership, the Laboratory of Renaissance Studies was successfully launched as a joint scientific project of the Shevchenko Institute of Literature (National Academy of Sciences of Ukraine, Kyiv) and Classical Private University (Zaporizhzhya). In 2009, the Ukrainian Shakespeare Centre was established and rapidly became the central Ukrainian academic institution in the domain of Shakespearian studies. Five international Shakespeare conferences (2009, 2010, 2011, 2014, and 2016) have been carried out by the centre, with proceedings published in two scientific journals: *Renaissance Studies* and *Shakespeare Discourse*. Both periodicals have gained recognition in Ukraine and abroad. In cooperation with the Union of Ukrainian Women in the United States, the centre established an annual competition for Shakespeare research papers written by young Ukrainian scholars.

To promote acquaintance among the wider scientific community with the Ukrainian Shakespearian discourse, *The Ukrainian Shakespeare Portal*[6] was created. Being the first attempt at a multimedia representation of Ukrainian Shakespearian studies, the site includes a selection of articles on Shakespeare-related issues (written in Ukrainian, Russian, and English), Ukrainian translations of the Bard's drama and poetry, and an extensive database concerning the Ukrainian reception of Shakespeare's legacy. The creators of the site are sure that "going online is one of the ways to prove Shakespeare is not just modern and relevant, but is at the very…cutting edge today."[7]

---

6 *The Ukrainian Shakespeare Portal.* shakespeare.in.ua/uk/.
7 Daria Lazarenko. "We Were Intrigued to Learn that Zaporizhzhia, the Sixth-Largest City in Ukraine, Is Home to the Exciting Academic and Cultural Venture That Is the Ukrainian Shakespeare Center". *Shakespeare Magazine.* 2017. www.shakespearemagazine.com/2017/05.

The story of the World Literature Department (initially the Department of Western European Literature) at Ivan Franko National University of Lviv began in 1939[8]. Its scholarly achievements within the first decades of the Soviet-Ukrainian period are associated with the leadership of two prominent professors and literary scholars: Mykhailo Rudnytskyi (1889–1975), who specialized in Ukrainian literature and comparative literary studies, and Oleksii Chicherin (1899–1989), whose books, specifically, *Ideas and Style*, and *Rhythm of the Image*, became the theoretical basis for the literary school dealing with the author's writing style. In the 1940s through the early '80s, Mariya Shapovalova (1915–94), author of the book *Shakespeare in Ukrainian Literature* (1976), laid the foundations of English studies at the department.

From 1985 to 1996 the World Literature Department was led by Albina Havryliuk, the specialist in John Galsworthy's oeuvre. Due to her efforts, English literature as well as German, French, and Spanish national literature has become obligatory academic disciplines. In-depth study of Western European national literature supplements generalizations made about the main literary trends that are delivered in lecture courses on the history of world literature. Despite the fact that the main achievements and literary personalities are included in programs of both basic courses offered, a new approach to teaching world literature has brought positive results. Students have been given the opportunity to get closely acquainted with a holistic coverage of English literature in its historical sequence, accompanied with knowledge about analogous phenomena in other Western European literature. After implementation of the Bologna Process standards in Ukrainian universities in 2005, a number of special (elective) courses, in particular, on the history of the English novel, British and Irish modernism, and the main trends in contemporary Anglophone literatures have been delivered to students at the bachelor's and master's degree levels.

---

8   The first university in this city was founded in 1661 by King John II Casimir of Poland (Polish: Jan II Kazimierz Waza). During 1919-39, Jan Kazimierz University of Lwów was the third largest Polish university (after the universities of Kraków and Warsaw). In the 1920s and '30s, English literary studies as well as studies in literary theory were successfully conducted within the humanities. In 1939, this university was re-created as Ivan Franko National University of Lviv.

In recent decades, scholarly work on Anglophone literature from the department has mostly covered the sphere of 20th century British and Irish literature. In particular, the monographs *David Lodge's Novels and Academic Context* (1998) and *Modernism between Past and Future: Anthropological Discourse of the English Modernist Novel* (2014) by Olha Bandrovska, and a textbook *Irish Modernism of the Late 19th and First Half of the 20th Centuries: William Butler Yeats and James Joyce* (2011) by Iryna Senchuk are noteworthy.

The main research activities over recent years in Ukrainian Anglistics have been focused on 20th century British and American literature. It is this vector of research that has been confirmed by Bandrovska's (2015) doctoral thesis in philology titled "Anthropological Discourse of the English Modernist Novel" and Miroshnychenko's (2016) thesis titled "Projections of Scepticism in Modern British Novel: Genesis, Traditions, and Poetics," which has also been defended. These following doctoral theses that still need to be defended also highlight this current research interest: "The English Historiographical Novel of the Turn of the 20th–21st centuries" by Boinitska and "Paradigmatics of the Lyric and Epic in Ezra Pound's *Cantos*" by Alexander Gon.

To conclude, over the course of the last few decades, notable but insufficient changes have taken place both in the study and teaching Anglophone literature in Ukraine. Both external and internal problems with higher education have slowed the development of academic freedom and independent scholarship. Unlike the government of independent Ukraine, scholars know the value of Thomas Jefferson's following words: "If a nation expects to be ignorant and free, in a state of civilization, it expects what never was and never will be."[9]

At the same time, despite the challenges that have been faced during recent years, including insufficient resources, excessive bureaucracy, and corruption, Ukrainian scholars across different generations have remained committed to researching the most fundamental and topical issues concerning the study of Anglophone literature. Like all the country's scholars, they are conscious that Ukraine's emphasis on the European world is

---

9   Merrill D. Peterson, *Thomas Jefferson and the New Nation: A Biography*, (Cary, North Carolina, USA: Oxford University Press, 1986), p. 145.

beyond dispute nowadays. Intellectually and spiritually, national literary studies as well as national literature can only exist in open spaces with dialogical intercultural connections. Consequently, today it is impossible to expect more scholarly development of English and American literary studies in Ukraine without integration into the European philological community.

Bibliography

Conversations of Goethe with Eckermann and Soret. Trans. John Oxenford. Vol. 1. London: Smith, Elder & Co, 1850. https//archive. org/stream/conversationsofg01goetuoft (15 February 2018).

Hassan, Ihab. "What Was Postmodernism and What Will It Become?". In: *20th Century American Literature after Midcentury. International Conference Proceedings*, ed. Tamara Denysova. Kyiv, 2000, pp. 9–18.

Lazarenko, Daria. "We Were Intrigued to Learn that Zaporizhzhia, the Sixth-Largest City in Ukraine, Is Home to the Exciting Academic and Cultural Venture That Is the Ukrainian Shakespeare Center". *Shakespeare Magazine.* 2017. https//www.shakespearemagazine. com/2017/05/ (15 February 2018).

Павличко, Соломія. "Насильство як метафора (Дискурс насильства в українській літературі)". In: Павличко, Соломія. *Теорія літератури.* Київ: Видавництво Соломії Павличко "Основи", 2002. https//lit. wikireading.ru/37080 (15 February 2018).

Peterson, Merrill D. *Thomas Jefferson and the New Nation: A Biography.* Cary, North Carolina, USA: Oxford University Press,, 1986.

"Philological Education in the USSR". In: *The Great Soviet Encyclopedia*, 3rd ed., 1970–79, Gale Group, Inc., 2010. https// encyclopedia2.thefreedictionary.com/Philological+Education+in+the+ USSR (15 February 2018).

The Ukrainian Shakespeare Portal. https//shakespeare.in.ua/uk/ (15 February 2018).

Soňa Šnircová

Literary Studies in English in Slovakia

Abstract: The present chapter offers an overview of the history and post-1989 developments of the literary studies in English at Slovak Universities. It provides the information about the study programmes that include Anglophone literature courses and covers the fields of specialisation developed by scholars in the English Departments throughout Slovakia. The chapter also presents an overview of major publications of Slovak Anglicists and maps their contribution to the international academic discussion about literary-critical and theoretical aspects of Anglophone literary production.

Keywords: Anglophone literature, Slovak universities, study programmes, Slovak Anglicists, major publications

Literary Studies in English at the Universities in Slovakia

When the Slovak Republic gained its independence in 1993, Josef Olexa observed that the unfavourable conditions which had prevailed in the past had left Slovak Anglistics with a short history and almost no tradition.[1] The history of English Studies in the Slovak part of the former Czechoslovakia started in the 1920s when the eminent Czech Celtist Josef Baudiš offered the first courses at Comenius University in Bratislava. After Baudiš' death the distinguished Czech scholar Otakar Vočadlo continued his work and together with other Czech and Slovak scholars, including František Kalda, Ján Šimko, Lev Soudek, Jozef Olexa, Josef Vachek, formed and made substantial contributions to the history of the contemporary Department of British and American Studies at the Faculty of Arts. The second centre of English Studies in Slovakia was established at the University of Pavol Jozef Šafárik, in the Faculty of Arts in Prešov in 1959. At first the study of Anglistics in Prešov fell under the auspices of a number of integrated departments; the Department of Western Philologies (1966–1968), the Department of Western Languages (1968–1975), and the Department of

---

1   Štefan Baštín, Jozef Olexa, Zora Studená, *Dejiny anglickej a americkej literatúry* [History of English and American Literature] (Bratislava: Obzor, 1993), p. 8.

German, English and Romance Studies (1980–1990). The foundations of the discipline in Prešov were also laid with the significant help of Czech scholars, primarily Milan Svěrák, Josef Jařab, Michal Frank, Ludmila Urbanová, Anna Grmelová, Josef Grmela.

The rapid development of English Studies in Slovakia started after 1989 when the collapse of the authoritarian regime created a more favourable atmosphere for the study of western philologies. The boom in English Studies since the establishment of the Slovak Republic has led to the current presence of ten English Studies departments across Slovakia: the Department of British and American Studies in the Faculty of Arts at Comenius University, Bratislava; the Institute of British and American Studies in the Faculty of Arts at the University of Prešov; the Department of English and American Studies in the Faculty of Arts at the Constantine the Philosopher University in Nitra; the Department of English and American Studies in the Faculty of Arts at Matej Bel University in Banská Bystrica; the Department of English Language and Literature in the Faculty of Arts and Letters at the Catholic University in Ružomberok; the Department of British and American Studies in the Faculty of Arts at the University of ss. Cyril and Methodius in Trnava; the Department of English Language and Literature in the Faculty of Humanities at the University of Žilina; the Department of British and American studies in the Faculty of Arts at Pavol Jozef Šafárik University in Košice; the Department of English Language and Literature in the Faculty of Education at Trnava University; and the Department of English Language and Literature in the Faculty of Education at Comenius University.

Literary studies in English form an integral part of all of the programmes offered by these departments. Prior to 1989, the study of the English language and English literature was an option which was only available within teacher training programmes, but Slovak universities now offer a variety of programmes that include studies in Anglophone literatures. *Teacher Training for Teachers of English Language and Literature* programmes are taught at all English departments and compulsory courses in British and American literatures usually form one third of the syllabus of these study programmes in combination with linguistic and cultural studies courses. The Slovak Accreditation Commission, an advisory body responsible for monitoring and evaluating the quality of education and research, prescribe a number of core courses in English Studies programmes which include literary theory, the history of Anglophone literatures and modern literary trends. The main aim of the courses is to help students acquire sufficient knowledge of literary-critical terminology, canonical texts and recent trends in Anglophone literatures and to develop students' skills in textual analysis and interpretation of literary texts.

Other programmes in which literary studies in English also play an important role are the study programmes which specialise in translation and interpretation. Such programmes include courses in *English Language and Culture* offered by Comenius University in Bratislava, Matej Bel University in Banská Bystrica and the University of Prešov; *English for European Institutions and Economics* offered by Pavol Jozef Šafárik University in Košice; specialisation in British and American studies: *English Studies* programme at Constantine the Philosopher University in Nitra; *British and American Studies* at the Pavol Jozef Šafárik University; and *English Language and Anglophone Cultures* at the University of Prešov. Literary courses within the British and American studies specialisation usually emphasize intersections between literary and cultural studies; literature is studied within wider socio-historical contexts, and analyses of literary texts focus on ideological issues connected with various cultural, ethnic, and gender-based approaches. Further specialisation in this respect is offered within the *Gender Studies and Culture* programme at the Pavol Jozef Šafárik University in which courses on literary representations of gender politics form a crucial element of the syllabus.

The compulsory courses of similar literary programmes offered by Slovak universities display a certain degree of homogeneity, primarily due to the need to incorporate the "core" topics prescribed by the Accreditation Commission into each course. However, the elective courses which are offered provide the opportunity for greater thematic variety. The elective literature courses offered by individual departments reveal their tendency to specialize in certain fields which include Canadian literature (Comenius University; Matej Bel University, the Catholic University in Ružomberok), Australian literature (the University of Prešov), postcolonial literature (Constantine the Philosopher University, Matej Bel University), feminist and postfeminist literature, gender politics in literature, American ethnic literatures, young adult literature, and detective fiction (Pavol Jozef Šafárik University).

The history of Canadian Studies[2] started in 1995 when the Department of British and American Studies at Comenius University organized the first meeting of Central European Canadianists in Budmerice. Interest in the field continued to grow and resulted in the establishment of the *Central European Association for Canadian Studies* in 2003 and the further development of scholarly activities with a focus on Canadian literature. One of the most prolific translators of Canadian literature into Slovak is Marián Gazdík whose research interests include Canadian short fiction of the 1950–1960s and the work of Barry Callaghan, Margaret Laurence and Leon Rooke. He has edited and acted as the main translator of the first anthology of Canadian short stories in Slovak entitled *Tichá hudba: antológia anglicko-kanadských poviedok* [Silent Music: An Anthology of Anglo-Canadian short stories].[3] Marián Gazdík's colleagues Mária Huttová and Lucia Otrísalová have also made significant contributions to the development of Canadian literary studies in Slovakia through their research into the work of Margaret Atwood, Michael Ondaatje, Alice Munro (Huttová) and Lawrence Hill and contemporary African-Canadian drama (Otrísalová). Jana Javorčíková from Matej Bel University has explored Canadian literature in the Slovak context and her work entitled "Kanadská literatúra v slovenskom preklade na začiatku nového milénia" [Canadian Literature in Slovak Translations at the Beginning of New Millennium][4] provides one of the most comprehensive studies of the critical reception of Canadian literature in Slovak. Katarína Labudová at the Catholic University of Ružomberok has also

---

2 I would like to express my gratitude to Professor Jaroslav Kušnír whose article "Postcolonial studies in Slovakia and Hungary" and whose personal mail communication have helped me to collect information about the activities of Slovak Anglicists in the field of Canadian, Australian and postcolonial studies.

3 Marián Gazdík, *Tichá hudba: antológia anglicko-kanadských poviedok* [Silent Music: An Anthology of Anglo-Canadian Short Stories] (Bratislava: Juga, 2000).

4 Jana Javorčíková, "Kanadská literatúra v slovenskom preklade na začiatku nového milénia" [Canadian Literature in Slovak Translations at the Beginning of New Millennium], in: *Preklad a tlmočenie 8*, eds. Mária Hardošová, and Zdenko Dobrík (Banská Bystrica: UMB, 2009), pp. 54–59.

actively pursued research in Canadian Studies, placing a special focus on the work of Margaret Atwood. Her colleague, Katarína Kaščáková, is a notable Slovak specialist in the works of the New Zealander Katherine Mansfield.

The University of Prešov is the unofficial centre of Australian studies in Slovakia, and the importance of its position was recognized by the European Association for Studies on Australia (EASA) when they chose to hold their *EASA 11th Biennial International Conference* in Prešov in 2011. Jaroslav Kušnír, the leading Slovak scholar in the field, has been pursuing research on postmodern and contemporary authors such as Peter Carey, Murray Bail and Richard Flanagan, and the results of his work are presented in his book-length study entitled *Australian Literature in Contexts*.[5] His academic interests include postcolonial theory and the representation of cultural identity in Australian literature and his work has also addressed the critical reception of Australian literature in Slovakia.

Postcolonial literary studies have been the focus of study at Constantine the Philosopher University in Nitra. Simona Hevešiová, Mária Kiššová and Alena Smiešková from the Department of British and American Studies have focused their research on the works of British Afro-Caribbean, Afro-American and Asian-American authors. Along with Anton Pokrivčák, they established *Ars Aeterna* in 2009, a journal which has become a critical platform for promoting research in postcolonial studies. Their activities include the organization of the *Aspects of Postcolonial Literature Conference* in 2006 and the publication of the results of their research in the books *Cultural Encounters in Contemporary Literature*[6] and *Multicultural Awareness: Reading Ethnic Writing*.[7]

Literary studies in English at the Pavol Jozef Šafárik University in Košice have been developed in a close interdisciplinary connection with gender and cultural studies. The Gender Studies and Culture programme that the University has offered since 2011 is the only programme in Slovakia

---

5   Jaroslav Kušnír, *Australian Literature in Contexts* (Banská Bystrica: Trian, 2003).
6   Simona Hevešiová, Mária Kiššová, *Cultural Encounters in Contemporary Literature* (Nitra: Filozofická fakulta UKF, 2008).
7   Alena Smiešková, Simona Hevešiová, Mária Kiššová, *Multicultural Awareness: Reading Ethnic Writing* (Nitra: Filozofická fakulta, UKF, 2008).

that focuses systematically on the representation of gender identities and feminist and postfeminist issues in British and American literature. The programme was designed with the help of international experts in the field whose close cooperation with Slovak literary scholars based at the University's Department of British and American studies resulted in the publication of the full-length study *Gender in Literature*.[8] Soňa Šnircová, Zuzana Buráková and Silvia Baučeková have actively contributed to the department's new focus by making gender issues the central concern of their research interests. Soňa Šnircová has explored gender politics in the works of British female authors, specialising in Angela Carter, the female grotesque and feminist and postfeminist trends in young adult literature. Zuzana Buráková, a specialist in trauma studies, has concentrated on gender issues in American-Jewish literature and Silvia Baučeková has searched for intersections between literary, gender and food studies in British and American women's literature. At the same time, these scholars are concerned with the most recent trends in theoretical discussions that reflect the "post-postmodernist" sensibility in Anglophone literature. A major achievement in this respect was the *Postmillennial Sensibility in Anglophone Literatures, Cultures and Media* conference held in Košice in 2017. The conference brought together international experts from twelve different countries and created a platform for truly interdisciplinary discussions.

Literary Studies in Major Publications by Slovak Anglicists

Prior to 1993, book-length publications on Anglophone literature by Slovak authors were rare, or indeed almost non-existent. Since the first English departments to be established in the Slovak part of the former Czechoslovakia were founded and developed under the guidance of Czech Anglicists, Slovak students were largely reliant on books on British and American literatures published by Czech authors (Stříbrný, Oliveriusová, Vančura, Jařab). These books, written in Czech, focus predominately on the history of English and American literatures, since at that time the

---

8 Nieves Pascual Soler, Ján Gbúr, eds, *Gender in Literature. Rod v literatúre* (Košice: UPJŠ, 2013).

courses on canonical works in historical and cultural contexts represented the main (or often the only) form of literary studies available in university programmes in western philologies.

Although English studies in Slovakia experienced decades of stagnation due to the communist regime's hostile attitude towards western cultures and languages, the first major work by Slovak authors that dealt with literature in English was published in the 1960s. The work took the form of several chapters which Ján Šimko, Zora Studená and Jozefína Janáková contributed to the book *Dejiny svetovej literatúry* [History of World's Literature][9] in which they discussed the history and development of British and American literatures. Slovak students had to wait a further thirty years before another major work on the history of British and American literatures written by Slovak authors appeared. *Dejiny anglickej a americkej literatúry* [A History of English and American Literature] by Štefan Baštín, Jozef Olexa and Zora Studená was published in 1993.[10] The establishment of the independent Slovak Republic lead not only to a significant increase in the number of departments of English studies in Slovak universities but also encouraged the research efforts of Slovak Anglicists which has in turn resulted in an increased rate of publications. Although the last twenty-five years have seen a considerable number of valuable studies on Anglophone literatures (both in terms of books and articles) published in Slovak, in general Slovak Anglicists have written their major studies in English and thereby joined the international forum of academic discussion.

Anton Pokrivčák's study *Americká imaginácia* [The American Imagination] works with the premise that "no work of art has a sense unless it expresses an impulse of the love for truth, which is [...] the actual meaning offered by the work for its readers."[11] Pokrivčák sees his book as an attempt to "show how this meaning is currently 'handcuffed' to the larger

---

9   Milan Pišút, Pavol Výraštek, eds, *Dejiny svetovej literatúry* [History of World's Literature] (Bratislava: Osveta, 1963).

10 Štefan Baštín, Jozef Olexa, Zora Studená, *Dejiny anglickej a americkej literatúry* [History of English and American Literature] (Bratislava: Obzor, 1993).

11 Anton Pokrivčák, *Americká imaginácia* [The American Imagination] (Nitra: Univerzita Konštantína Filozofa, 2005), p. 119.

social and cultural issues of today, resulting in the establishment of a new discourse referred to as 'theory.'"[12] The theoretical section of Pokrivčák's work critically addresses poststructuralist theoretical discourses and postmodern trends in western criticism. Pokrivčák recognizes the positive effect of the "theory" and its "fresh insights into the nature of literary understanding" and its potential to enlarge "the limits of aesthetic perception."[13] On the other hand, he believes that the theory's saturation with "sociological trends to *political correctness* broke the fragile 'dialectics' between the universal and the particular, which has been one of the most valuable features of art, and open the way for a language of proliferated political agenda of various interest groups (women, minorities)."[14] He suggests that in order to reconnect literary theory to the universal, it is necessary to refocus on the ontological aspects of literary works. The focus on the ontological is understood as "the exploration of an individual response to the world of the work as well as the analysis of a point of contact with *the other*. And as such, it would be primarily existential. It manifests itself in the validity of the work's impact on the reader's life, channelled through the process of reception" (italics in the original).[15]

Pokrivčák explores the ontological using selected examples from American literature; a literature which, as he claims, has long been informed by a strong sense of existential otherness, from its Puritan origins to the contemporary trends of postmodernism. He analyses the works of R.W. Emerson, N. Hawthorn, H. Melville, E. Dickinson, W. Stevens and J. Irving and bases his interpretations within the theoretical framework of New Criticism. New Criticism is defended against the accusations of reductionism, ahistoricism and mechanical spiritless formalism on the basis of its actual deep interest in the aesthetic-philosophical dimensions of literature.[16] With the help of Allan Tate's works, Pokrivčák demonstrates that the formalistic and structuralist approaches of New Criticism are primarily concerned with the exploration of specific meanings of literary

---

12 Pokrivčák, *Americká imaginácia*, p. 119.
13 Pokrivčák, *Americká imaginácia*, p. 119.
14 Pokrivčák, *Americká imaginácia*, p. 119.
15 Pokrivčák, *Americká imaginácia*, p. 120.
16 Pokrivčák, *Americká imaginácia*, p. 30.

texts that are studied in the wider context of human existence. Pokrivčák's own analyses of major works from the American literary tradition are intended as a contribution to the critical reception of literature in which concern with the metaphysical and transcendental meanings of literary texts prevail over the (potentially) nihilistic relativization of all meanings.

The book *Literature and Culture* by Anton Pokrivčák et al. is a result of the authors' "joint effort to reflect upon current tendencies in literary studies in a complex way, exploring both new potentialities for the interpretation of literary works as well as point out certain drawbacks."[17] In the chapter "Multiculturalism, Transcendentalism and the Fate of American Literature," Anton Pokrivčák reflects on the (correct and welcome) rise of multicultural awareness in American literary criticism and expresses his concern about the potential dangers that this trend holds for the study of literature. He draws attention to Gregory Jay's distinction between a "proper" multiculturalism that respects the diversity of American "common" culture and a "dangerous" form that undermines and/or rejects the concept of common culture.[18] He uses this as the starting point for a discussion of the need to approach "the principles of studying literature through 'cultural studies'" with caution.

Pokrivčák draws a parallel with the politics of socialist realism and maintains that cultural studies' approaches to literary texts also run the risk of overpoliticizing literature. The overemphasis on the political and ideological aspects of literature by various ethnic and other cultural groups undermines the need to explore the common aesthetic and thematic elements that are shared by literary texts in all their ethnic and other variations. This spoils "the charm of the study of literature" which lies in "finding what connects people, not what separates them."[19] In support of his case, Pokrivčák discusses the American transcendentalist movement as an indisputably Eurocentric tendency in American culture, but one which is not necessarily "in conflict with current multicultural trends."[20] He focuses on Emerson's work as the main connecting element between the

17 Anton Pokrivčák et al., *Literature and Culture*. (Nitra: UKF, 2010), p. 7.
18 Pokrivčák et al., *Literature and Culture*, p. 10.
19 Pokrivčák et al., *Literature and Culture*, p. 30.
20 Pokrivčák et al., *Literature and Culture*, p. 16.

European literary heritage and American new "independent" literature as represented by such authors as Whitman and Dickinson. The main thrust of his argument is that although American transcendentalism is often seen as being embedded in " 'Eurocentric' conceptions of art," critics tend to forget that its major proponents such as Emerson "could not be called literary nationalists."[21] Pokrivčák sees Emerson's 'internationalism,' reflected in his interest in Eastern (especially Persian and Indian) thinking, as "a fact that his legacy is complex and cannot be associated only with Western influences."[22]

In her book *Mýtus. Realita. Rozprávanie. Philip Roth.* [Myth. Reality. Narrative. The Case of Philip Roth], Alena Smiešková makes use of postmodern critical thought (Frederic Jameson, Jean-Fracois Lyotard, Jean Baudrillard, Charles Jencks, Linda Hutcheon, Brian McHale) to outline the cultural sensibility and aesthetics that shaped the character of Philip Roth's work. The author explores Roth's specific position in American ethnic literatures and offers a concise study of a selection of Roth's writings that document his creative transition from modernism to postmodernism. Smiešková notes that Roth's classification as an American-Jewish author does not fully reflect the complexity of his work. Although the connection between his works and Jewish culture is strong, his specific usage of self-reflexive irony has also earned him accusations of anti-Semitism.[23] Smiešková's analyses of Roth's works explore the "recursive structures" in his narratives which are aimed at questioning transethnic issues such as "the nature of reality, art and the writer's mission."[24] She sees Roth's major contribution to American literature as his foreshadowing of "the pluralisation of the American literary canon" and his contribution to the "dehierachization of American culture."[25]

Jaroslav Kušnír's *American Fiction: Modernism-Postmodernism, Popular Culture, and Metafiction* explores the boundaries between

---

21 Pokrivčák et al., *Literature and Culture*, p. 28.

22 Pokrivčák et al., *Literature and Culture*, p. 29.

23 Alena Smiešková, *Mýtus. Realita. Rozprávanie. Prípad Philip Roth* [Myth. Reality. Narrative. The Case of Philip Roth] (Nitra: Univerzita Konštantína Filozofa, 2011), p. 26.

24 Smiešková, *Mýtus. Realita. Rozprávanie*, p. 142.

25 Smiešková, *Mýtus. Realita. Rozprávanie*, p. 142.

modernism and postmodernism through his discussion of narrative strategies in the works of Donald Barthelme, E.L. Doctorow, Richard Brautigan, Paul Auster, Kurt Vonnegut and Robert Coover. Kušnír's analysis of the works of Robert Coover forms the backbone of the book and places particular emphasis on Coover's postmodernist appropriations of traditional genres such as the western, pornography and fairy-tales. Kušnír perceives Coover's parody of the western genre as "a form of cultural criticism" that treats the myth of the American frontier as an illusion.[26] Coover's questioning of false heroism is seen as his criticism of the glorification of the national mythology which has played such a major role in the construction of American identity.[27] On the other hand, Coover's appropriation of the genre of pornography and his use of images of physical and sexual violence are interpreted as his "critique of the use and misuse of power" in the tradition of Western cultural discourse.[28] Kušnír also notes that Coover creates a pornographic atmosphere only in order to subvert it and thus create a "playful and parodic vision of reality" that suggests a criticism of commercialism, consumerism, and traditional conservative values.[29] Finally, Coover's rewritings of such traditional fairy-tales as *Sleeping Beauty, Pinocchio, Beauty and the Beast* or *Little Red Riding Hood* present, in Kušnír's opinion, the author's unmasking of the artificiality and falsehood of mythical and folkloric narratives and his critique of the system of traditional values that these narratives embody.

Postmodernist rewritings of traditional literary forms is also the main topic of Soňa Šnircová's *Feminist Aspects of Angela Carter's Grotesque*, which is intended as a contribution to the study of the grotesque genre and its feminist appropriations. The book explores Angela Carter's novels in the framework of the theory of the grotesque (Mikhail Bakhtin, Wolfgang Kayser, Arthur Clayborough, Peter Stallybrass and Allon White) and feminist, poststructuralist and postmodernist theories (Julia Kristeva, Luce Irigaray, Judit Butler, Michel Foucault, Linda Hutcheon). Bakhtin's

---

26 Jaroslav Kušnír, *American Fiction: Modernism-Postmodernism, Popular Culture, and Metafiction* (Stuttgart: Ibidem Verlag, 2005), p. 54.
27 Kušnír, *American Fiction*, p. 77.
28 Kušnír, *American Fiction*, p. 78.
29 Kušnír, *American Fiction*, p. 87.

distinction between a positive, liberating carnivalesque grotesque and a negative, dark Romantic grotesque is used to examine important changes and continuities in Carter's poetics which had developed over the thirty years of her creative life. In Šnircová's reading, Carter uses grotesque aesthetics to demonstrate that female and male subjectivities are constructed by patriarchal discourses and to express her concern with the problematic position of the female subject in the Lacanian symbolic order that is permeated by patriarchy's ambivalent attitude to the female body.

Šnircová further maintains that "like Bakhtin in his study of Rabelais, Carter in her novels foregrounds such grotesque elements as grotesque body, grotesque degradation of the high and grotesque motifs of the mask, puppet and madness. However, she combines these elements with a category that Bakhtin ignores, the category of gender, and thus creates her own specific contribution to the development of literary grotesque."[30] Šnircová also addresses Tibor Žilka's categorization of the grotesque into Renaissance, Romantic, modernist and postmodernist subcategories and claims that this categorization cannot easily be applied to "Carter's feminist appropriation of the grotesque."[31] On the one hand, Carter's grotesque is postmodernist since her novels present the imitation and reinterpretation of the traditional types of the grotesque that is typical of postmodernist literature. However, "it cannot be really defined as the postmodernist grotesque that 'reinterprets everything through the prism of irony' and that 'rejects definiteness, completeness, but above all, progressivity.'"[32] While the ironic postmodernist grotesque results in a "playfulness that does not foreground a clear ideological position," Carter's grotesque, in Šnircová's view, foregrounds the political agenda of feminism.[33]

Šnircová's second book-length study, *Girlhood in British Coming-of-Age Novels. The Bildungsroman Revisited*, explores the feminist and postfeminist transformations of another literary genre – the classic Bildungsroman. The book adopts the theoretical approaches of feminist criticism which had

---

30 Soňa Šnircová, *Feminist Aspects of Angela Carter's Grotesque* (Košice: UPJŠ, 2012), p. 21.
31 Šnircová, *Feminist Aspects*, p. 112.
32 Šnircová, *Feminist Aspects*, p. 112.
33 Šnircová, *Feminist Aspects*, p. 113.

delineated the female version of the classic Bildungsroman (Elizabeth Abel, Marianne Hirsch, Elizabeth Langland) and the feminist Bildungsroman (Rita Felski), a product of second wave feminism. Šnircová discusses a selection of coming-of-age narratives to map the development of the girl heroine under the influence of the Bildungsroman tradition (Jane Austen, Charlotte Brontë) and the influence of feminist and postfeminist cultural trends in post-war and postmillennial Britain. She argues that feminist transformations of female maturation narratives have been so far concerned mainly with adult female protagonists (the feminist Bildungsroman). Šnircová instead places her focus on the post-war girl heroine (Dodie Smith's *I Capture the Castle*, Rummer Godden's *The Greengage Summer*, and Jane Gardam's *Bilgewater*) which allows her to "examine coming-of-age narratives in which second wave feminist concerns, the fight for gender equality in private and public spheres of life, the role of female solidarity in the process of women's emancipation and the victim status of women in patriarchy, coexist with the centrality of heterosexual romance in the heroine's life."[34] The fact that these narratives explore the possibilities of female emancipation in the context of a heterosexual partnership means that they are "more consistent with the classic female Bildungsroman tradition than the feminist Bildungsroman with its tendency to exclude heterosexual romance from the successful process of female maturation."[35]

In contrast, Šnircová's discussion of the postmillennial girl heroine (Tiffany Murray's *Happy Accidents,* Caitlin Moran's *How to Build a Girl, Helen Walsh's Brass*, Susan Fletcher's *Eve Green*) reflects on the effect of popular media images of women on literary narratives about girlhood. She examines neoliberal postfeminist tendencies (Girl Power, new traditionalism, the rejection of victim feminism) in the representations of girl's coming-of-age in these four novels to question their role in postmillennial developments of the female Bildungsroman genre. On the basis of her in-depth analyses, Šnircová concludes that these novels do not present a simple rejection of feminist politics but rather work within the oscillation

---

34 Soňa Šnircová, *Girlhood in British Coming-of-Age Novels: The Bildungsroman Heroine Revisited* (Newcastle upon Tyne: Cambridge Scholars Publishing, 2017), p. 32.

35 Šnircová, *Girlhood*, p. 32.

between feminist and postfeminist perspectives on the female situation in the western postmillennial world.

Jaroslav Kušnír's book *Postmodernism and After: New Sensibility, Media, Pop Culture, and Communication Technologies in Anglophone Literatures* discusses works of David Foster Wallace, Steve Tomasula, Chuck Palahniuk, Robert Coover, Richard Powers, Gerald Vizenor and Tom Cho. These works represent a new sensibility that is seen as a reaction against the postmodern aesthetic and philosophical trends that have lost their former innovative and creative potential, a result of their institutionalization and commercialization.[36] The first part of the book focuses especially on Wallace's short fiction and explores the author's representations of the world of the media, communication technologies and pop culture through "meta-metafictional" narrative strategies.[37] Kušnír notices that Wallace's work combines critical images of contemporary commercialized culture with the parody of the postmodern writings by older generation of postmodernists (John Barth, Thomas Pynchon, Donald Barthelme, William Gass).[38] The second part of the book presents analyses of selected narratives by American, Native American and Chinese Australian authors to illustrate the various ways in which the new sensibility is represented in contemporary Anglophone literatures. Kušnír finds in these works a strong tendency to combine the criticism of negative effects of consumerist, media and technology driven culture with the attempts to find new (post-postmodernist, post-metafictional) "ways of truthful and spontaneous representation of human experience and communication."[39]

Silvia Baučeková's *Dining Room Detectives. Analysing Food in the Novels of Agatha Christie* is the comprehensive result of her research in literary, food and gender studies. The book explores the role of food in Agatha Christie's crime fiction, concluding that it serves as a literary device

---

36 Jaroslav Kušnír, *Postmodernism and After: New Sensibility, Media, Pop Culture, and Communication Technologies in Anglophone Literatures* (Nitra: ASPA, 2015), p. 5.

37 Kušnír, *Postmodernism and After*, p. 13.

38 Kušnír, *Postmodernism and After*, p. 34.

39 Kušnír, *Postmodernism and After*, p. 163.

which Christie uses "to tackle issues of identity, crime, or memory."[40] Baučeková uses a structuralist theoretical framework and draws on structuralist scholars' understandings of the formulaic nature of crime fiction and their perception of food as a cultural sign with symbolic meanings. She stresses the structural similarities between cooking a meal according to a recipe and writing a novel according to a classic detective formula and points out how this similarity relates to a strongly feminine aspect of Christie's work. The study argues that Christie makes frequent reference to food "thanks to its strong association with women, femininity and domesticity," which "enabled her to feminize an otherwise inherently masculine form of writing: the detective story."[41] The book also makes use of feminist, phenomenological, psychoanalytic and cultural studies theories to explore Christie's treatment of identity, class and nation. Baučeková again stresses the important role of food imagery in Christie's work which, she maintains, "helped [Christie] to mock, satirise, and eventually transgress the norms and values of the society she depicted in her novels."[42]

The effort of Slovak Anglicists to participate in a broader academic discussion on literatures in English and offer their perspectives on western literary criticism has also been reflected in their major contributions to publications by international teams of experts. Janka Kaščáková's paper "'Ironing-because-its-Tuesday': Significant Presences and Absences in Katherine Mansfield's 'How Pearl Button Was Kidnapped'" addresses the predominant critical approaches to Mansfield's short story. She points out that this story about the kidnapping of a girl by Maori women has mainly provoked feminist readings that focus on the girl's "liberation" from the power structures of her white patriarchal culture. Kaščáková offers an alternative reading and polemizes with the scholars who, in her opinion, have failed to consider fully "the peculiarities of the child's perspective"[43]

---

40 Silvia Baučeková, *Dining Room Detectives: Analysing Food in the Novels of Agatha Christie* (Newcastle upon Tyne: Cambridge Scholars Publishing, 2015), pp. 2–3.

41 Baučeková, *Dining Room Detectives*, p. 10.

42 Baučeková, *Dining Room Detectives*, p. 182.

43 Janka Kaščáková, "'Ironing-because-its-Tuesday': Significant Presences and Absences in Katherine Mansfield's 'How Pearl Button Was Kidnapped'," in: *Presences and Absences: Transdisciplinary Essays*, eds. Nóra Séllei and

that Mansfield uses in her narrative. She pursues an interesting argument carefully considering and undermining the unambiguous validity of interpretations of the short story that work with clear-cut distinctions between the restrictive and insincere white society and the supposedly more natural society of the Maori. Her analysis challenges the interpretation of the story as "an allegorical journey towards freedom of choice and expression,"[44] instead identifying "Mansfield's double irony," the author's ironic criticism of "idealistic theories of childhood her contemporaries cherished so much" and her implicit criticism of the idealization of the Maori as "noble savages."[45]

In her work "Waterless Flood and Mythless Myth: Absence/Presence of Biblical Myths in Oryx and Crake (2003) and The Year of the Flood (2009) by Margaret Atwood," Katarína Labudová also declines to focus on the "obvious aspect of feminism" which can be found in the analysed texts but instead concentrates on their "more general (post)humanist concerns."[46] She draws on Northrop Frye's myth criticism, Jack Zipes' Fairy Tale as Myth: Myth as Fairy Tale and Roland Barth's Mythologies to discuss "the paradoxical process of de-mythifying and re-mythifying"[47] in Atwood's narratives. She argues that "Atwood returns to the Biblical myth of the flood to question its vitality as well as the ethical capacities of humankind."[48] On the basis of her close reading analysis of the two apocalyptic novels, Labudová focuses on "gaps" and "blank absences" in the narratives that she reads as the "doors open for the imagination and what if speculation"(italics in the original).[49] She relates Atwood's focus on myth to the author's awareness of the archetypal human dependence

Katarína Labudová (Newcastle-upon-Tyne: Cambridge Scholars Publishing, 2013), p. 172.

44 Kaščáková, "Ironing-because-its-Tuesday," p. 175.

45 Kaščáková, "Ironing-because-its-Tuesday," p. 184.

46 Katarína Labudová, "Waterless Flood and Mythless Myth: Absence/Presence of Biblical Myths in Oryx and Crake (2003) and The Year of the Flood (2009) by Margaret Atwood," in: Presences and Absences: Transdisciplinary Essays, eds. Séllei Nóra and Labudová Katarína (Newcastle-upon-Tyne: Cambridge Scholars Publishing, 2013), p. 220.

47 Labudová, "Waterless Flood and Mythless Myth," p. 220.

48 Labudová, "Waterless Flood and Mythless Myth," p. 220.

49 Labudová, "Waterless Flood and Mythless Myth," p. 229.

on mythological structures of thinking and belief systems and sees the author's narrative strategies as an opportunity for the reader to "identify possible harmful effects" of both religious and secularized myths.[50]

Contemporary literature by women authors is also the focus of Silvia Baučeková's work "Cooking Her Up: Renegotiating the Kitchen in Four Stories of Female Development." The work explores the possibilities offered by the interdisciplinary connections between literary and food studies. With the use of feminist theory (Betty Friedan, Julia Kristeva, Susan Bordo) and major works on the Bildungsroman genre (Franco Moretti, Marianne Hirsch, Lorna Ellis), Baučeková discusses a selection of four American novels to explore the crucial role that food plays in the development and identity formation of the female protagonists. Baučeková's interpretations of Betty Fussell's *My Kitchen Wars*, Aimee Bender's *The Particular Sadness of Lemon Cake*, Amy Tan's *The Joy Luck Club* and Julie Powell's *Julie and Julia* present a response to the feminist backlash argument about the reactionary nature of new traditionalism promoted by the postfeminist media. In her reading, the selected narratives show that the private space of the kitchen can be reclaimed as a place in which women can "embrace their womanhood, form meaningful relationships with others, and achieve satisfaction within (and beyond) their socially prescribed role."[51] Baučeková suggests that women's escape from confinement to the kitchen and their separation from the traditional role of nurturer may not be so easy (and may not even be so desirable) as is expected by second wave feminists. In her view, the novels' protagonists' physical and sensual engagement with food, cooking, and eating appears not only as a form of empowerment but also as a means of closing the gap between the traditional binaries: masculine/feminine, private/public, life/death, and this process can be seen as an important step in the characters' journeys "towards maturity and self-acceptance."[52]

---

50 Labudová, "Waterless Flood and Mythless Myth," p. 226.
51 Silvia Baučeková, "Cooking Her Up: Renegotiating the Kitchen in Four Stories of Female Development," in: *Growing up a Woman: The Private/Public Divide in the Narratives of Female Development*, eds. Soňa Šnircová and Milena Kostić (Newcastle upon Tyne: Cambridge Scholars Publishing, 2015), p. 336.
52 Baučeková, "Cooking Her Up," p. 353.

Zuzana Buráková's work "Double Trouble: Female *Bildung* in Jewish American Fiction: Anzia Yezierska's *Bread Givers*" offers a similar exploration of specific aspects of female development, but the main thrust of the work focuses on the literary representation of the Bildung process in American ethnic literature. Buráková starts from the premise that the wide variety of ethnicities that shape American literature have rendered the original Eurocentric definition of Bildugsroman (as defined by Wilhelm Dilthey, Jerome Buckley and Franco Moretti) no longer sufficient. The maturation process in the ethnic Bildungsroman is more complex than the traditional white middle-class Bildung narratives imply. The Ethnic Bildungsroman includes "several relationship trajectories: the formation of the relationship of the individual towards their own ethnic group, the relationship of the ethnic towards mainstream society and lastly the relationship between different ethnic groups."[53] Buráková uses a close reading analysis of Yezierska's novel to explore how the "multiple consciousness" of the female protagonist complicates the process of her identity formation. She argues that the female protagonist, who struggles to be a daughter, a woman, a Jew and an American, appears to be stranded in "what Homi K. Bhabha calls 'the third space'–neither one nor the other but forever in between."[54]

Jaroslav Kušnír's contribution to *A Companion to Australian Literature Since 1900* is confirmation of the recognition of his expertise in Australian studies by the international academic community. His chapter presents a concise overview of the postmodernist trends in the works of Michael Wilding, Murray Bail, Rodney Hall, and Frank Moorhouse. Kušnír connects the literary achievements of these authors with the particular fact that "their familiarity with contemporary tendencies in the development of literature and literary criticism, as well as with Australian literary

---

53 Zuzana Buráková, "Double Trouble: Female *Bildung* in Jewish American Fiction: Anzia Yezierska's *Bread Givers*," in: *Growing up a Woman: The Private/Public Divide in the Narratives of Female Development*, eds. Soňa Šnircová and Milena Kostić (Newcastle upon Tyne: Cambridge Scholars Publishing, 2015), p. 149.
54 Buráková, "Double Trouble," p. 155.

and artistic tradition, have enabled [them] to redirect the trajectory of Australian fiction since the 1960s."[55]

This outline of Slovak Anglicists' major contributions to book publications by international research teams can be concluded with Soňa Šnircová's chapter "Dickens in Slovakia" published in the volume *The Reception of Charles Dickens in Europe*.[56] The chapter maps the publication and critical reception of Dickens' works in Slovakia from the first translation of Dickens into Slovak in 1895 to the most recent production of Ján Cikker's opera *Mister Scrooge* at the Slovak National Theatre in Bratislava in 2011. Šnircová reveals that the earliest Slovak criticism of the work of Dickens (and of Shakespeare) had appeared in the work of the one of the very first distinguished Slovak literary critics, Svetozár Hurban Vajanský, whose discussion of the English author was published in 1866 in the Slovak region of the Austro-Hungarian Empire.[57] Although these initial remarks on the English authors were brief and were more concerned with Vajanský's interest in the revival of Slovak national culture, they nonetheless prove that the importance of English literature has been recognized in Slovak literary criticism from its very origins. After more than one hundred and fifty years that have passed since the first remarks on Dickens and Shakespeare,[58] it is safe to conclude that Slovak studies in English literature have undergone a major development and acquired a prominent position in literary-critical writing in Slovakia.

Bibliography

Baštín, Štefan, Jozef Olexa, Zora Studená. *Dejiny anglickej a americkej literatúry* [History of English and American Literature]. Bratislava: Obzor, 1993.

---

55 Jaroslav Kušnír, "Michael Wilding, Murray Bail, Rodney Hall, and Frank Moorhouse," in: *A Companion to Australian Literature since 1900*, eds. Nicholas Birns and Rebecca McNeer (Rochester, NY: Camden House, 2007), p. 345.
56 Soňa Šnircová, "Dickens in Slovakia," in: *The Reception of Charles Dickens in Europe*, ed. Michael Hollington (London: Bloomsbury Publishing, 2013).
57 Šnircová, "Dickens in Slovakia," p. 467.
58 I completed the survey of Slovak literary studies in English in 2017.

Baučeková, Silvia. "Cooking Her Up: Renegotiating the Kitchen in Four Stories of Female Development." In: *Growing up a Woman: The Private/Public Divide in the Narratives of Female Development*, eds. Soňa Šnircová and Milena Kostić. Newcastle upon Tyne: Cambridge Scholars Publishing, 2015, pp. 334–356.

Baučeková, Silvia. *Dining Room Detectives: Analysing Food in the Novels of Agatha Christie*. Newcastle upon Tyne: Cambridge Scholars Publishing, 2015.

Buráková, Zuzana. "Double Trouble: Female *Bildung* in Jewish American Fiction: Anzia Yezierska's *Bread Givers*." In: *Growing up a Woman: The Private/Public Divide in the Narratives of Female Development*, eds. Soňa Šnircová and Milena Kostić. Newcastle upon Tyne: Cambridge Scholars Publishing, 2015, pp. 145–158.

Gazdík, Marián. *Tichá hudba: antológia anglicko-kanadských poviedok* [Silent Music: An Anthology of Anglo-Canadian Short Stories]. Bratislava: Juga, 2000.

Hevešiová, Simona, Mária Kiššová. *Cultural Encounters in Contemporary Literature*. Nitra: Filozofická fakulta, UKF, 2008.

Hilský, Martin. *Současný britský román* [Contemporary British Novel]. Praha: H & H, 1992.

Jařab, Josef, et al. *Antologie americké literatury* [Anthology of American Literature]. Praha: Státní pedagogické nakladatelství, 1985.

Javorčíková, Jana. "Kanadská literatúra v slovenskom preklade na začiatku nového milénia" [Canadian Literature in Slovak Translations at the Beginning of New Millennium]. In: *Preklad a tlmočenie 8*, eds. Mária Hardošová, and Zdenko Dobrík. Banská Bystrica: UMB, 2009, pp. 54–59.

Kaščáková, Janka. " 'Ironing-because-its-Tuesday': Significant Presences and Absences in Katherine Mansfield's 'How Pearl Button Was Kidnapped.' " In: *Presences and Absences: Transdisciplinary Essays*, eds. Nóra Séllei, Katarína Labudová. Newcastle-upon-Tyne: Cambridge Scholars Publishing, 2013, pp. 171–186.

Kušnír, Jaroslav. *Australian Literature in Contexts*. Banská Bystrica: Trian, 2003.

Kušnír, Jaroslav. *American Fiction: Modernism-Postmodernism, Popular Culture, and Metafiction*. Stuttgart: Ibidem Verlag, 2005.

Kušnír, Jaroslav. "Michael Wilding, Murray Bail, Rodney Hall, and Frank Moorhouse." In: *A Companion to Australian Literature since 1900*, eds. Nicholas Birns and Rebecca McNeer. Rochester, NY: Camden House, 2007, pp. 345–358.

Kušnír, Jaroslav. "Postcolonial Studies in Slovakia and Hungary." *Porównania: Czasopismo Poswiecone Zagadnieniom Komparatystyki Literackiej Oraz Studiom Interdyscyplinarnym*. Vol. 17, no. 17, 2015, pp. 245–252.

Kušnír, Jaroslav. *Postmodernism and After: New Sensibility, Media, Pop Culture, and Communication Technologies in Anglophone Literatures.* Nitra: ASPA, 2015.

Labudová, Katarína. "Waterless Flood and Mythless Myth: Absence/ Presence of Biblical Myths in *Oryx and Crake* (2003) and *The Year of the Flood* (2009) by Margaret Atwood." In: *Presences and Absences: Transdisciplinary Essays*, eds. Séllei Nóra, Labudová Katarína. Newcastle-upon-Tyne: Cambridge Scholars Publishing, 2013, pp. 219–233.

Oliveriusová, Eva, ed. *Dějiny anglické literatury* [History of English Literature]. Praha: Státní pedagogické nakladatelství, 1988.

Pascual Soler, Nieves, Ján Gbúr, eds. *Gender in Literature. Rod v literatúre*, Košice: UPJŠ, 2013.

Pišút, Milan, Pavol Výraštek, eds. *Dejiny svetovej literatúry* [History of World's Literature]. Bratislava: Osveta, 1963.

Pokrivčák, Anton. *Americká imaginácia* [The American Imagination]. Nitra: Univerzita Konštantína Filozofa, 2005.

Pokrivčák, Anton, et al. *Literature and Culture*. Nitra: UKF, 2010.

Smiešková, Alena, Simona Hevešiová, Mária Kiššová. *Multicultural Awareness: Reading Ethnic Writing*. Nitra: UKF, 2008.

Smiešková, Alena. *Mýtus. Realita. Rozprávanie. Prípad Philip Roth* [Myth. Reality. Narrative. The Case of Philip Roth]. Nitra: Univerzita Konštantína Filozofa, 2011.

Stříbrný, Zdeněk. *Dějiny anglické literatury* [History of English Literature]. Praha: Academia, 1987.

Šnircová, Soňa. *Feminist Aspects of Angela Carter's Grotesque.* Košice: UPJŠ, 2012.

Šnircová, Soňa. "Dickens in Slovakia." In: *The Reception of Charles Dickens in Europe*, ed. Michael Hollington. London: Bloomsbury Publishing, 2013, pp. 466–475.

Šnircová, Soňa. *Girlhood in British Coming-of-Age Novels: The Bildungsroman Heroine Revisited*. Newcastle upon Tyne: Cambridge Scholars Publishing, 2017.

Vančura, Zděnek. *Dvacet let anglického románu 1945-1964* [Twenty Years of English Novel]. Praha: Academia, 1976.

Madalina Nicolaescu

Managing the Devaluation of English Literature Studies in Romanian Universities

Abstract: This chapter takes a critical look at internal and external, transnational factors shaping university studies in Romania and will argue that one of their consequences has been the erosion in scope and importance attached to English literature. The chapter first considers the curricular homogeneity in teaching English literature at university level and searches its causes in the very mechanisms of Romanian higher education system. Past and present constraints are shown to contribute to this situation. The second part of the chapter looks at curricular diversification and development of English literature studies. A final subsection discusses the author's own experiences in teaching Shakespeare.

Keywords: curricula in English literature, Bologna process, isomorphism and accreditation institutions, diversification of curricular offers

I. Curricular Homogeneity

In Romania, like in the other former countries of the socialist bloc, the teaching of English literature raises interesting questions regarding continuities and dis-continuities in vision and organization of education with the previous socialist period. The paradigm shift brought about by the integration of Romanian universities within the Bologna process has further strongly impacted the study of English literature. This chapter will take a critical look at internal and external, transnational factors shaping university studies in Romania and will argue that one of their consequences has been the erosion in scope and importance attached to English literature. Though English literature continues to be the subject of literature core courses organized by English departments across the country, it has lost much of its pre-1989 aura and, despite concentrated efforts on behalf of the academia, it keeps losing ground.

I will pursue my argument starting from answers to questionnaires sent to academics teaching English literature in major public and private universities, which are further supplemented with interviews of students in the English Department of the Bucharest University. In the first part of the chapter I will provide a general evaluation of mechanisms in the Romanian higher education system that can be put down as the major sources for the striking curricular homogeneity in teaching English literature at university level. Past and present constraints are shown to contribute to this situation. The second part of the chapter will look at curricular diversification and development, including the author's own experiences in teaching Shakespeare.[1]

The questionnaires I have sent to the English departments indicate the persistence of the organizational structures set up in the socialist period. The centralized system of Romanian tertiary education has not been subjected to a major overhaul, even if universities have gained a certain degree of autonomy.[2] Unlike in Poland or the Czech Republic, the attempt to devolve power to departments and chairs has not been very successful and authority and control are still vested with the Ministry.[3] While curricula are no longer designed within the Ministry of Education, they are still subject to the approval of a central accreditation institution. The Ministry continues to provide the overarching framework and vision of higher education institutions down to the organization of academic disciplines. The effect is that the former homogeneity in teaching core courses and in structuring the content of education has been reproduced. All departments across the country follow the same pattern and change seldom occurs following pressure from below.

The major reforms that the Bologna process initiated in Romanian higher education, paradoxically reinforced the previous homogeneity. The accreditation institution (ARACIS), which was supposed to assure certain quality standards in universities and bring them in line with western institutions, has imposed "a coercive and mimetic isomorphism" in tertiary

---

1   The data employed in this study were collected over the period 2015–2016.
2   Jan Sadlak, *Transnational Education and the New Economy*. (Paris: European Centre for Higher Education – UNESCO, 2001).
3   For a comparison between the higher education systems in Romania versus Poland and the Czech Republic, see Michael Dobbins, *Higher Education Policies in Central and Eastern Europe: Convergence towards a Common Model*. (New York: Palgrave Macmillan, 2011), pp. 20–23, 94–98, 194–197.

education.[4] Emerging or even established universities have had to conform to the standards imposed by the accreditation procedure or to copy the strategies developed by the more powerful and successful institutions, for fear of being either excluded or marginalized. Innovative or alternative approaches have thus often been discarded: for example, the private universities which had previously departed from the established pattern of chronological approaches to literature and offered courses on Shakespeare in the last academic year, when students have acquired the linguistic and cultural skills necessary for these studies, have had to abandon this approach and conform to the general pattern, unproductive though it may be. The general environment for teaching core courses in English literature favours conformism rather than promoting innovation and change.[5] The previous system has thus been largely reproduced, innovative strategies in organizing or in redesigning core courses in literature (involving more student-centred interaction or the use of mass- and multimedia) have not been encouraged by the new evaluation and accreditation procedures.

The pressure for homogeneity and isomorphism has further been increased by the combined factors of the massification of higher education and its chronical underfunding. While the number of students has dramatically increased over the past two decades, higher education has been chronically underfunded. Even nowadays it is allotted the lowest funds per student in the EU., i.e. below 1500 euros.[6] Expenditure on education is below 3% of the GDP, which places Romania in the last place among European countries. While the average percentage of the GDP allocated to higher education in the EU was around 1.3, it only amounted to 0.7 % in Romania. "Expensive" forms of higher education involving small groups of students who are encouraged to carry on debates in class and to submit frequent written assignments for which they get ample feed-back

---

4   Bogdan Florian, Iulia Gheorghiu, Adrian Miroiu, Lazar Vlăsceanu. *Barometrul Calității 2010. Starea calității in învățământul superior din România.* Bucureşti: Agenția Română de Asigurare a Calității în Învățământul Superior, 2010), pp. 25–27.

5   Mihai Păunescu, Adrian Miroiu, Lazar Vlăsceanu. *Calitatea învățământului superior din România.* (Iaşi: Polirom, 2011), pp. 57–58.

6   EUROSTAT. https://ec.europa.eu/eurostat/statistics-explained/index.php?title= Tertiary_education_statistics

have either been abandoned or not introduced at all. As the major concern of universities has been to survive in dire financial conditions rather than develop and innovate, what is favoured are more mass oriented approaches that focus on conveying large amounts of information to large numbers of students.[7] This accounts for the persistent importance attached to survey courses in teaching English literature at the expense of more interactive strategies of teaching.

The recent "paradigm shift" in Romanian higher education towards a market-oriented vision that involves both the endeavour to meet the exigencies of the market economy and the adoption of entrepreneurial strategies has not been favourable to the development of literary studies. [8] The introduction of a market-based logic in higher education has increased the marginalization of the humanities and the arts that had already started in the socialist period. Though not officially acknowledged, the study of English literature had enjoyed a high cultural and social prestige in the socialist period, as it signified an opening towards western culture and offered the possibility to carry out a dialogue across the Iron Curtain. Nowadays neither the market nor the university seem to have identified any particular social or cultural need for teaching English (or American) literature. The combined pressures of positivism and of market-oriented pragmatism place the study of all foreign literatures in a difficult position. Their predicament is compounded by the fact that the studies of foreign literatures, unlike that of Romanian literature, cannot be easily appropriated to nationalist agendas either. The dominant trend towards an uncritical acceptance of the logic of the marketplace and the excessively pragmatic evaluation of English studies in terms of the jobs that they can secure has had far-reaching negative effects upon the study of English literature.

Radical changes in the curricula of secondary school studies of English, the content of the school leaving examinations included, has practically evacuated English literature from the pre-university system. The requirements for entrance examination to English departments have been modified correspondingly. If previously students preparing for this

---

7 Paunescu, *Calitatea învăţământului*, p. 57.
8 Dobbins, *Higher Education Policies*, p. 101.

exam were expected to go through a relatively wide selection of literary texts (including excerpts from Shakespeare's *Julius Cesar* or from novels by Henry James, Joseph Conrad and Thomas Hardy), now they can be admitted to the university without having had any exposure to English literature at all. The evacuation of English literature in secondary schools has made the articulation with higher education difficult.[9] Academics feel they must start from scratch, while the goal they aim at is to bring their students to levels of knowledge, understanding and critical thinking similar to those achieved in Anglophone countries.

The diminishing social relevance attached to English literature has affected higher education institutions as well. Cultural studies programmes have practically displaced the traditional subjects associated with English (read British) literature at MA level. An MA program centred on English literature set up at the University of Bucharest in 2000 managed to survive only three years. The students' demand was very low, as the completion of the program was not perceived to translate in skills or a kind of cultural capital that was in demand on the labour market. On the other hand, more practice-oriented MA programmes centred on strategies of translation have been thriving. In almost all the MA programmes organized by the English departments across the country, literature subjects are introduced "under cover," as an unacknowledged component of the cultural studies profile. Shakespeare, for example, is taught as part of a course on film adaptations.

Furthermore, the erosion of the importance of English literature (read British literature) is associated with the increasing interest in other literatures in English: American literature has made the greatest curricular in-roads, displacing English literature courses, which are now limited to the first two academic years. Courses on Scottish and Irish literature were the first to be included within the umbrella of "cultural studies" of MA programs. More recently, Australian, South African and South East Asian literatures have emerged as centres of interest within MA studies at the Bucharest and Cluj universities.

---

9   On the gap between pre-university education and the requirements of higher education, see Florian, *Barometrul calității*, p. 15.

II. Sources for Diversification of Literature Courses

The re-organization of higher education required by the Bologna process has dealt the study of English literature a heavy blow. Prior to the
Bologna reform, English literature used to be taught over a period of at
least six semesters (many universities extended it to seven semesters). The
re-organization of higher education in a two-tiered structure (three years
of undergraduate studies and two of graduate studies) has meant that the
study of English literature is restricted to four semesters at the University of
Bucharest and five semesters at the other universities. English departments
tried to oppose this change, yet the Ministry had a strong leverage over
higher education institutions and completed the Bologna process scoring
six excellent grades out of eight.[10]

The Romanian universities organize the teaching of English (British)
literature in the form of core courses that display the same format: two
hours of survey lectures per week coupled with two-hour seminars every
second week.[11] The survey courses are all organized along the same lines –
they are centred on authors and tackle literature in a chronological order.
This means that students, irrespective of their proficiency in English, are
first exposed to medieval literature, Chaucer and the Renaissance, mostly
Shakespeare. An emerging university ("Dimitrie Cantemir") attempted to
gauge the content of the literature courses to the linguistic skills of its
students and placed the Shakespeare courses in the last term. However,
under pressure to obtain accreditation, it copied the dominant pattern and
abandoned its "innovation," reverting to the chronological organization.

Mention must also be made that Romanian universities, excepting the
small local ones, provide programs in two foreign languages leading to a
double specialization. This involves a double working load for students,
yet it increases the level of their graduate employability. English literature

---

10 Silvia Florea, Peter J. Wells, "The Bologna Process Reforms" in *Higher Education in Romania*. (Bucharest: CEPES – UNESCO, 2011), pp. 52–63. By comparison, the Czech Republic has posed a strong resistance to the attempts at convergence via the Bologna Process. See Dobbins, *Higher Education Policies*, p. 194.

11 The one exception is the English Department of the University of Iaşi which has managed to negotiate the increase of seminar hours for English literature to two hours per week.

is therefore taught alongside another foreign language literature, which on the one hand limits the scope and the centrality attached to English literature and on the other hand offers students the possibility to carry a dialogue between English and other literatures.

What is the content and structure of the English literature studies? Given the chronological approach of these studies, first-year students start with the medieval and Renaissance literature, with great emphasis on Shakespeare's plays read in the original version. The syllabus of the second term concentrates on 18th century literature and is impressive in both range and quantity of the reading material: it includes novels by Defoe, Fielding, Sterne, Swift, next to Pope's *Essay on Man* and the *Rape of the Lock,* pre-romantic poetry (Blake, Thomsen, Gray) as well as romantic poetry (Coleridge, Wordsworth, Shelley, Byron and Keats). Lectures provide a general survey and a historical contextualization of the period, while the seminars discuss fragments from the novels or poems included in the bibliography. The syllabus of the third term is just as impressive as it tackles major 19th century novelists (Dickens, Eliot, Hardy, the Bronte sisters and Oscar Wilde), next to the essays of Carlyle and John Stuart Mill and the poetry of Browning and Tennyson. A conspicuous absence is Jane Austen. Back in the 1960s she was considered a minor writer, whose work did not rise up to the standards that socialist criticism had imposed on realist literature. The fact that she has not been included in the syllabuses of English departments despite the Austen mania of recent times is indicative of the extent to which present curricula reproduce the previous socialist ones.[12] The sixth academic term is devoted to 20th century literature: survey courses start with poetry (Yeats, Eliot), the modernist novel (Joyce, Woolf and Conrad) and end with post-war novelists (David Lodge, Ishiguro, Fowles). The third year (i.e. semesters five and six) is generally devoted to the study of American literature. The University of Bucharest has dared to depart from the established pattern and resumes study of Shakespeare for another term in the third year, albeit under cover, as it

---

12 The English Department of the University of Cluj has introduced a strong gender dimension to the study of the 18th and 19th century novel and discusses not only Jane Austen but also minor authors such as Eliza Haywood and Charlotte Turner Smith.

were. The course is not formally considered to be on "literature" but is viewed as an extension of the "British civilization" series.

As far as critical bibliography is concerned, it varies from teacher to teacher. Though the list of bibliographical titles is quite generous, students are expected to rely mostly on the information provided during the lectures and seminars. According to the responses provided in the interviews, students feel pressured for time and carry out little independent work. As the survey courses place emphasis on information, the students' creative participation is elicited mostly during the seminars which focus on the close reading of texts. However, as the reading load for a double specialization is heavy and a large part of the students do not manage to go through the material in advance, the teacher must revert to information-centred strategies to provide the missing links. Such situations often leave little room for discussions and affect the students' development of critical skills and of the capacity to produce alternative readings of their own.

The insistence on the diffusion of information at the expense of the development of skills can be viewed as a strategy to cope with the massification of education: the seminars group together large numbers of students who have had little training in dealing with texts and have limited background information. At the same time, the readiness to supply more data during seminars could be related to a general anxiety to provide students with as much information as possible. This partially carries over from the socialist period when access to specialized information was very limited and academic teachers perceived it their mission to impart the treasured material to their students.

Another effect of the massification and commercialization of higher education coupled with underfunding is the limited amount of writing that students are expected to produce for the literature courses. The highly overworked and grossly underpaid academic staff cannot muster up the energy to correct papers coming from increasingly larger numbers of students. The questionnaires have shown that the students of the English Department of the University of Bucharest produce on average two or three independent essays over the period of three years; most of their contribution in class consists of "oral presentations," which is often a compilation of sources found in the critical bibliography or on the internet.

The teaching of English literature can therefore be said to be deficient in the development of critical spirit and narrative imagination, the two competences that Martha Nussbaum particularly praises about the study of foreign languages at university level.[13] Too little scope is devoted to close readings and creative debates that are conducive to the expansion of imagination and to the development of a reflexive awareness of the differences in culture that the study of English literatures involves. Nor does the approach to literary texts insist on the difference to be made between the perspective of a home-grown student of English literature and that of a Romanian student, who looks at the respective texts with a different set of values and expectations.[14] The Romanian academics tend to identify themselves with the positions of Anglo-American critics which they disseminate in their courses and do not insist on working out the differences in critical perspective entailed by their own cultural embedding. There is too little emphasis on the cultural translation and cultural negotiations inherent in reading English literature in a different geo-cultural space. Though post-colonial approaches are discussed and adopted in the study of contemporary novels, there is hardly any attempt at placing English literature in relationship with the rather marginal, subaltern position of Romanian culture. The limited use of mass media (film adaptations, YouTube productions) in class is further indicative of the reluctance to embed the study of English literature within the global visual culture of the present.[15]

---

13 Martha Nussbaum, *Not for Profit. Why Democracy Needs the Humanities.* (Princeton and Oxford: Princeton University Press, 2010). For a Romanian perspective on this issue, see also Andrei Marga "Values of the University" in eds. Jan Sadlak, Klaus Hufner, Remus Pricopie and Laura Grunberg, *Topical Contributions and Outcomes – UNESCO Forum on Higher Education in the Europe Region: Access, Values, Quality and Competitiveness.* (Bucharest: CEPES, 2009), pp. 152–172.

14 Teaching English literature to Romanian students could benefit from recent approaches to teaching World Literature; see David Damrosch, *How to Read World Literature.* (Oxford: Wiley–Blackwell, 2007).

15 The answers to the questionnaire given to students in the English department in Bucharest indicate a limited use of multimedia products in the core courses, which tend to be text- and print-centred.

III.

The rigid educational system from the previous period was loosened up in the nineties, when the introduction of the so called optional/elective courses gave students more choice and teachers more freedom in both content and approaches. The optional (elective) courses are provided as a supplement that can lend more flexibility and diversity to the system as students must select two out of a basket of about ten courses offered to them. This process of "diversification in the margins" has been the most innovative trend in teaching English literature in Romanian universities. There has been a constant competition within the academic community of English departments across the country to offer courses that provide ever more attractive and up-to-date topics and theoretical approaches. It is here that lines of study derived from gender studies, post-colonial studies, ethical criticism and eco-criticism, or from cognitive sciences have been introduced. It is the optional courses that broach novel subjects such as transnational literature, hyphenated or diasporic writers. The titles are also more attractive than those of the core courses and challenge entrenched taboos in Romanian canonical approaches, such as gender constructions in 19th century fiction, sex and violence in Shakespeare. They often offer new vistas of study such as the course on the intellectual history of imagination in the pre-romantic period which adopts a cognitive approach to emotions and moral judgements. New conjunctions are forged between literature and media studies (film, TV and comics), literature and cultural anthropology or various philosophical trends. One of the most successful courses discusses the rise of modernity by looking at 18th century popular culture, including best seller novels. As the boundary between literary studies and cultural studies is highly fluid and permeable in these courses, they pave the ground to the approaches at MA level, where literature has nominally disappeared. Most of the optional courses cover topics related to recent research projects that the staff members have been involved in and offer students the opportunity to indirectly participate in the respective research work, thereby bridging the gap between research and learning.

Though the optional courses do not have seminars attached to them, the level of interactivity is much higher than in the core courses. Teachers and students (in much smaller numbers than those attending the core courses) constitute themselves in small communities of study, with teachers sharing their bibliographical resources and discussing their ongoing research with the students. Most of the subjects for the students' future diploma papers are selected from among the topics broached within the special courses. The individualized interaction and close relationship between students and academics are thus continued over a longer period of study.

The English departments in Iaşi and Timişoara have expanded the integration of innovative courses in the core curricula and have upgraded some of the optional/elective courses as alternatives to the core courses themselves. The department in Iaşi has introduced an alternative stream for the third and fourth academic terms, called *The Theory and Practice of Language/the Text* which relies upon cultural studies informed approaches.[16] The courses discuss a series of 19th and 20th century literary texts (novels, poems) in conjunction with a selection of non-fictional texts, viewed as representative of the major ideological and cultural discourses of the respective periods. A course on film adaptations is also offered as a core course for the fifth term. The department at the University of Timişoara has introduced alternative core courses on topics that fully resonate with new concerns in theory and criticism, such as: theories of narrativity (with reference to the work of Marie Laure Ryan and David Hermann) applied to Victorian novels; harbingers and agents of postmodernism in the 20th and 21st century novel, and Victorianism and Neo-Victorianism, designed to reconsider the 19th and late 20th century novel.[17]

How do English departments cope with the difficulty of articulating secondary and tertiary education given the chronological organization of literature curricula which means that the study of English literature must start with medieval literature and Shakespeare? Given the exclusion of literature in secondary school classes, most students have almost no experience in reading literature in English. Quite a few have hardly ever heard

---

16 See Alexandru Ioan Cuza University, *Faculty of Letters-Study Guide: BA Programmes 2016–2017*, www.uaic.ro/wp-content/uploads/2013/12/StudyGuideBA2016. pdf, p. 35.

17 See the site of the Western University of Timişoara (Universitatea de Vest din Timişoara), https: //litere.uvt.ro/educatie/programe-de-licenta/colectivul-de-limba-si-literatura-engleza-limbi-si-literaturi/.

of another Shakespeare play beside *Romeo and Juliet* which they study in Romanian. The contact with Shakespeare is all the more traumatic as the plays have to be read in the original and recourse to translations is strongly discouraged. To make the nut easier to crack, extensive use is made of contemporary adaptations of the plays, coupling the study of the plays in the Oxford editions with film versions, YouTube clips and graphic novel versions. The goal is a double one – to enable access to Shakespeare via the global visual culture students are familiar with and to try to facilitate a dialogue with the past that the plays belong to. The success of the enterprise has been rather limited as students tend to dismiss both movies and graphic novels as popular culture, which they do not consider a fitting object of university study. The bias inculcated in secondary school against popular and visual culture has been hampering their access to Shakespeare. Another remedial action adopted is to couple close readings of Shakespeare's lines with corresponding lines in various Romanian translations of the respective play. The approach insists on the contextualization of the meanings in translation which are further contrasted with the meanings in Shakespeare's age. Such comparisons have proved to be a productive way to bridge the gap between the English early modern period and the concerns of present day students. Students are encouraged to grasp the historical dimension of the Romanian versions and to relate to the Shakespeare play without falling back on presentist readings. The awareness of multiple meanings in the Romanian translation makes them more open to the cultural differences inherent in the Shakespearean text.

The English department in Bucharest offers a second core course on Shakespeare in the fifth term. However, it is organized under the guise of "the study of British civilization" and is not officially registered as a literature course. The course relies heavily on a film studies approach which compares several adaptations of a given play. One of the goals of this course is to develop critical awareness of the discursive strategies and ideological positions inscribed in the various Shakespeare adaptations. However, though the course refers to the global media culture that students are immersed in, reading texts of visual culture critically has proved almost as difficult as understanding Shakespeare's dense and poetic texts.

The recent diversification of courses via optional/elective courses is just one example of the strategies Romanian professors employ to counteract the marginalization of the study of English literature. Diversification and changes in the established format of English literature core courses have given an important impetus to the general trend of rethinking the study of literature in the context of the post-Bologna environment. The general outlook is the more promising as it is the junior staff members that are mostly called upon to organize the diverse optional courses and who are further expected to carry out a major overhaul of the way English literature is taught in Romanian universities.

Bibliography

Alexandru Ioan Cuza University. "Faculty of Letters-Study Guide: BA Programmes 2016–2017." www.uaic.ro/wp-content/uploads/2013/12/StudyGuideBA2016.pdf (2 September 2017).

Damrosch, David. *How to Read World Literature*. Oxford: Wiley-Blackwell, 2007.

Dobbins, Michael. *Higher Education Policies in Central and Eastern Europe: Convergence towards a Common Model*. New York: Palgrave Macmillan, 2011, pp. 20–23, 94–98, 194–197.

Eurostat. "Statistics Explained". (2017). http://ec.europa.eu/eurostat/statistics-explained/index.php?title=Statistics_Explained. (15 August 2017).

Florea, Silvia and Peter J. Wells. *Higher Education in Romania*. Bucharest: CEPES -UNESCO, 2011, pp. 52–63.

Florian, Bogdan, Iulia Gheorghiu, Adrian Miroiu and Lazar Vlăsceanu. *Barometrul Calității 2010. Starea calității in învățământul superior din România*. Bucureşti: Agenția Română de Asigurare a Calității în Învățământul Superior, 2010, pp. 25–27.

Marga, Andrei. "Values of the University". In: *Topical Contributions and Outcomes – UNESCO Forum on Higher Education in the Europe Region: Access, Values, Quality and Competitiveness*, eds. Jan Sadlak, Klaus Hufner, Remus Pricopie and Laura Grunberg. Bucharest: CEPES, 2009, pp. 152–172.

Nussbaum, Martha. *Not for Profit. Why Democracy Needs the Humanities*. Princeton and Oxford: Princeton University Press, 2010.

Păunescu, Mihai and Adrian Miroiu, Lazar Vlăsceanu. *Calitatea învățământului superior din România*. Iaşi: Polirom, 2011, pp. 57–58.

Sadlak, Jan. *Transnational Education and the New Economy.*
Paris: European Centre for Higher Education-UNESCO, 2001.

Western University of Timişoara (Universitatea de Vest din Timişoara)
Facultatea de litere, Istorie si Teologie. "Programe de licenta: Limbi
şi Literaturi." 2016. https://litere.uvt.ro/educatie/programe-de-
licenta/colectivul-de-limba-si-literatura-engleza-limbi-si-literaturi/ (1
September 2017).

Mirko Jurak, ed. by Igor Maver

Shakespeare's Plays in Slovenia in the First Half of the 20th Century: The Case of Jakob Kelemina

Abstract: The article discusses the productions, translations and interpretations of William Shakespeare's plays in Slovenia in the first half of the 20th century and provides a brief overview of the development of Slovene theatre. The stress is then put on Jakob Kelemina's contribution to Shakespeare studies in the Slovene language, including especially the debate surrounding the poet's Oton Župančič's translations of some of Shakespeare's plays.

Keywords: Shakespeare, Slovenia, theatre, Kelemina

Introduction

Theatrical life in Slovenia has a long history, which dates back to the Renaissance period, even though for a long time it mainly depended on visits of foreign theatre groups, which came to Ljubljana quite regularly and performed Shakespeare's plays particularly in the 18th and 19th century. However, the students of the Jesuit College in Ljubljana, had occasionally also produced plays; so, for example, they staged in Ljubljana a German a version of the King Lear story already in 1698. However, the first play written in Slovene was *Škofjeloški pasijon* (1721), a religious procession text about the death of Jesus Christ. The beginner of Slovene drama, Anton Tomaž Linhart (1756–1795), was thrilled by Shakespeare's plays which he saw in Vienna and he even wrote a play *(Miss Jenny Love)* under Shakespeare's influence. The greatest Slovene poet, France Prešeren (1800–1849), was also familiar with Shakespeare's plays, but his friends were not able to persuade him to write a play on a historical theme, like Shakespeare.

Throughout the 19th century many Slovene authors and critics mention Shakespeare and his works in their essays and in their criticism. This is also the period when the first Slovene translations of individual scenes from Shakespeare's plays appeared in Slovene periodicals. After 1876 a number of Slovene professional theatre groups contributed to a very vivid theatrical life in Ljubljana and later on also in some other cities (Maribor, Trieste/Trst). Although in the 19th century several less known translators tried to make Slovene readers (and later on also audiences) acquainted with Shakespeare's plays, the most important contribution in this field was made by Oton Župančič (1878–1949), who translated eighteen of his plays. One of the main problems at the beginning of the 20th century was the lack of knowledge of English in Slovenia so that the majority of translators, including Župančič's first translations of Shakespeare's plays, were prepared on the basis of the German translations. This also resulted in many linguistic errors, which appeared in the early Slovene translations of Shakespeare's plays.

Jakob Kelemina (1882–1957) published his first book review of Župančič's translation of *The Merchant of Venice* in 1907. After the First World War he had already written two lengthy reviews of Župančič's translation of *Othello,* and of three Croatian translations of Shakespeare's plays. He pointed in his reviews to a number of grammatical, lexical and syntactical mistakes also in Župančič's translation, and advised him and Croatian translators to use for their translations the English originals. In 1920 Kelemina contributed an introductory essay and notes to Župančič's translations of *A Midsummer Night's Dream,* and in 1921 to *The Merchant of Venice* and to *Macbeth.* Kelemina's interpretations show his scholarly approach to Shakespeare's plays. In his introductions he discussed literary, historical, ethical, ethnographic and other aspects of Shakespeare's plays. In his meticulously prepared notes he offered abundant explanation of individual syntagms and passages in these plays. This, no doubt, helped Župančič in his translations of Shakespeare's plays. But from Župančič's letters and notes we can see that Kelemina's approach to these plays, which was more philologically oriented, did not suit the translator, and it is most likely that the differences in their characters did not help their cooperation either. It was stopped altogether after 1922, when Kelemina wrote his last review of Slovene and Croatian translations of Shakespeare's plays prepared by Oton Župančič, Milan Bogdanović and Milan Šenoa. Kelemina especially pointed out in this review that Župančič's translations were more poetic than the translations by the two above mentioned Croatian translators. It is not only the opinion of the

author of this chapter but also the opinion expressed by two most important translator's after Župančič, Matej Bor and Milan Jesih, that Župančič
indulged himself in the beauty of his poetic translations to such an extent
that he sometimes neglected to include in his translations the complexity of
meaning expressed by Shakespeare in his plays, so rich in poetic elements.
Bor's and Jesih's translations are thus much closer to everyday colloquial
speech. Kelemina was the first Slovene critic whose writings about Oton
Župančič's translations of Shakespeare's plays still have a scholarly value.
Jakob Kelemina helped Župančič in his work as a translator with practical
suggestions regarding the possibilities of translating indirectly, with his
theoretical views on drama and with his suggestions for Župančič's use
of literature on Shakespeare's plays, different interpretations and dictio-
naries to achieve a very high standard in his translations. Jakob Kelemina,
Professor at the then established University of Ljubljana, definitely also
set the standards for future interpretation and evaluation of Shakespeare's
plays in Slovenia through the twentieth and into the 21st century.

Jakob Kelemina

Among Slovene scholars in English and German studies Jakob Kelemina
(19 July 1882–14 May 1957) has a very important place. Janez Stanonik
justifiably places him among the founding fathers of the University of
Ljubljana.[1] From 1920 Kelemina was a Professor of Germanic philology
and between 1920 and 1957 also the Chair of the Department of Germanic
Languages and Literatures at the Faculty of Arts of this university. The
major part of Kelemina's research was devoted to German and Austrian
literatures, German philology, German-Slovene cultural relations, and literary theory; his work in these fields has already been discussed by several
Slovene scholars.

However, in the first two decades of the 20th century Kelemina also
wrote several book reviews of Slovene and Croatian translations of
Shakespeare's plays as well as three introductory essays to Slovene
translations of Shakespeare's plays. They are regarded as the first serious

---

1 Janez Stanonik, "Jakob Kelemina." in: *Pomurski zbornik* (Murska Sobota:
   Pomurska založba, 1966), p. 332.

studies on Shakespeare in Slovenia (Moravec 1974: 437), and have not
been analysed yet. Therefore this topic presents the core of this study,
together with an evaluation of Kelemina's contribution to Slovene
translations of Shakespeare's plays done by Oton Župančič (1878–1949)
during the first half of the 20th century. Župančič's translations became
the criterion for all further translations of Shakespeare's dramatic works in
Slovene. Župančič is still one of our most important poets and translators
of this time and Kelemina's advice and criticism undoubtedly also helped
him to achieve such a high standard in his translations.

With the establishment of the Dramatic Society (Dramatično društvo) in
Ljubljana in 1867, and of the same kind of societies in other cities (Trieste/
Trst, in 1902; Maribor, in 1909; Celje, in 1911), which all performed plays
only in Slovene, the repertoire of these theatre groups became comparable
to other important theatres in Europe. These were also the first professional
Slovene theatre companies and theatrical life in Slovenia was thus greatly
improved.[2] They all performed plays in Slovene and their performances
became, generally speaking, quite professional. The Dramatic Society in
Ljubljana was the forerunner of the Slovene National Theatre in Ljubljana
(Drama SNG v Ljubljani – SNG), and its founding represents the beginning of a continued activity of professional theatre in Slovenia. On 29
December 1899, the first Slovene performance of *Hamlet* was staged. The
play was originally translated by Dragotin Šauperl,[3] but when it was produced only the name of Ivan Cankar, who adapted the play, appeared

2   The information regarding the programme of Slovene theatres since 1867
is available in *Repertoar slovenskih gledališč. 1867–1967* (A Repertoire of
Slovenian Theatres. 1867–1967, published by the Slovenski gledališki muzej
in Ljubljana, 1967). The Slovene Theatre Museum also published subsequent
bibliographical compilations of the repertoire, at first every five years, titled
Dokumenti slovenskega gledališkega muzeja (Documents of the Slovene Theatre
Museum), and since 1993 yearly, under the title *Slovenski gledališki letopis*
(Slovene Theatre Annual). The latter publications are much more comprehensive
than the earlier bibliographies and include also data on actors, the number of
performances of plays and the number of theatre-goers, visits of different theatre
companies in other theatres and abroad etc. In my study I use the English titles of
these documents and of Slovene theatres, as they are given in these publications.
3   Dragotin Šauperl (1840–1869), a priest, translator. In 1865 he translated *Hamlet*
and soon afterwards also *King Lear*. His translation of *Hamlet* was so good that

on the theatre-bill as the translator of *Hamlet*. This was probably due to Cankar's high reputation as a poet, prose writer and dramatist. However, the first important Slovene translator of Shakespeare's plays became Oton Župančič (1878–1949), who translated into Slovene eighteen plays written by Shakespeare in the period between 1905 and 1949, the year of his death.

Oton Župančič was not only a fine poet but also a man who loved the theatre and went to see theatre performances whenever and wherever he could. However, in the final period of his life he wished he did not have so many administrative duties so that he could devote his life only to translating and writing. When he was a student he spent several years in Vienna and in Paris. Already in 1908 he proposed to the newly established publishing house and cultural centre, Slovenska matica, in Ljubljana, to translate some of Shakespeare's most important plays into Slovene. However, due to the First World War the project was postponed and the contract in which he obliged himself to translate about ten plays written by Shakespeare into Slovene was not signed until December 1919. Župančič also agreed in the contract that each play would have an introduction, and that for the reimbursement of the author of the critical study he would provide a fee out of the payment he got from the publishing house to translate into Slovene about ten plays written by Shakespeare.

Župančič often visited other countries where he saw productions of plays by some of the best theatre companies in Europe (e.g. besides performances in the Burgtheater and other theatres in Vienna he saw a number of performances at the Comédie Française in Paris, at the Narodni Divadlo in Prague, at various theatres in Italy etc.). Later on, in the thirties, he also went to see performances of plays done by the theatres in Norway and in England, and when he saw *The Taming of the Shrew* at Stratford-upon-Avon, he realized that it was not only the German theatres, which could perform Shakespeare's plays well, and thus the English theatre with its artistic perfection was a real revelation for him.[4] Oton Župančič was thus well-acquainted with the classical and contemporary European

---

Ivan Cankar did not have to do any major alterations but only brought it closer to Slovene literary language.

4   Joža Mahnič. "Župančič kot organizator in teoretik prevajanja." *Zbornik Društva slovenskih književnih prevajalcev*. Ed. Janko Moder (Koper: Založba

drama. In 1910, after his return from Vienna to Ljubljana, he began to write theatre reviews. Already at this time he was famous in Slovenia for his publications of lyric poetry and poetry written for children. In 1912–13 he became the stage manager of the Slovene National Theatre (Drama) in Ljubljana, and in 1920 he resumed this post. From 1929 he was also the general manager of this theatre, and in this function he combined the administrative duties and the duties of the artistic director. This position allowed him not only to choose the repertoire for this theatre, as he was also influential in other aspects of theatrical productions.

Oton Župančič's poetic rendering of Shakespeare's plays into Slovene for the Slovene National Theatre in Ljubljana (in the period between the two wars several of his translations of Shakespeare's plays were also performed in Maribor), definitely marks a new era in the Slovene theatre. Throughout his life Župančič saw Shakespeare's plays as "an ever-fixed mark" in the art of the theatre. Shakespeare was for him an icon, an ideal which was worth admiring and which he also hoped to reach in his own plays. This thought can be traced not only in the repertoire he chose for the Slovene National Theatre but also in his theatre reviews, his notes and in his prefaces in the playbills for performances of Shakespeare's plays in Slovenia as well as in his own dramatic attempts. He also regarded as one of the main tasks of the Slovene National Theatre to perform plays written by Slovene playwrights and classical drama, particularly Shakespeare's works, which, in his view, so "perfectly expressed real life." Župančič also believed that a "beautiful" translation, like that of Cankar's *Hamlet,* was essential for a good performance. In his view translations which are prepared by "craftsmen" (like Glaser) do not have an artistic value, because they lack the suggestive poetic power of the Bard. Župančič also disapproved of the contemporary naturalistic tendencies on the stage, the wish to create on the stage an illusion of reality, because this very idea was for him "an illusion," a gross deception of the theatre audience. He was not thrilled by modern presentations of *Hamlet* done in England (by Hamlet wearing a

---

Lipa, 1980), p. 9. Oton Župančič translated into Slovene – besides Shakespeare – also a number of plays written by other famous European authors (e.g. Hofmannsthal, Calderon, Voltaire, Molière, Rostand, Schiller, Ibsen, G. B. Shaw, Galsworthy etc.).

tail-coat, having a monocle and smoking cigarettes, but he did not oppose theatrical improvisations in plays like *The Taming of the Shrew,* in which Shakespeare's contemporary life is shown. For the *Comedy of Errors* he would even suggest the use of "passionless marionettes and their stylized movements," because they would not cheat the public with an appearance of reality. These "technicalities" linked with performing Shakespeare's plays in Slovene theatres, particularly in the Slovene National Theatre in Ljubljana, show Župančič as a rather moderate innovator in theatre productions. In Shakespeare's works he mainly saw the playwright's revelation of his ideas, his view of the world and his rediscovery of man's belief in his fellow-man, in secret higher powers that lead our lives with "celestial righteousness and grace," as he expressed himself in 1925 in his introduction in the playbill to *The Winter's Tale.* He believed that rationalistic probability was not quintessential for Shakespeare but that the dramatist wished to present in his plays real, complex world. In an interview which Župančič gave for the Slovene newspaper *Jutro* in 1927[5] he made his famous statement that *"Hamlet* is considered by the Slovenes as our best and most beloved popular (folk) play." The theatre was not for him only a place where his own translations were staged, it was for him a vital part of his daily life. His criticism of naturalistic tendencies, which were then practiced in various European theatres, was expressed by Župančič in his writings already in the early 1920s.

Kelemina's Introductions to Some of Shakespeare's Plays in the Slovene Translations by Oton Župančič: *Macbeth*

The plot and the theme of the play have attracted critics' attention to Shakespeare's presentation of the nature of evil and its embodiment in the central characters for centuries and therefore it is understandable that the central focus of Kelemina's criticism is oriented towards these questions. The play was published in 1921 in a Slovene translation prepared by Oton Župančič and edited by Tiskovna zadruga in Ljubljana. Kelemina wrote the Introduction (5–16) and Notes to the play (137–151), in which he mentions that the most recent critical works were not available to him.

---

5   "Oton Župančič o Shakespearu," Interview, *Jutro* 16 April 1927, 17.

He adds the glossary of the pronunciation of proper names and names of places and regions mentioned in the play, which was a novelty in his writings on Shakespeare's plays, and particularly valuable at the time of the appearance of Slovene translation of the play, when English was not yet *lingua franca* in Europe. Kelemina mentions that he used as a source for his Notes works written by two German scholars (G. Kohlmann and O. Thiergen). His Notes are substantial enough and explain not only historical facts mentioned in the play but also connotations implied in the text. There is one slip which he made with regard to Malcolm and Donalbain: they are not King Duncan's grandsons, as mentioned in note 7 to Act 1 *(Macbeth* 139), but his sons.

Kelemina deals in his remarks with literary and theatrical aspects concerning the play. He points out that the first published version of *Macbeth,* which appeared in 1623, is an unsatisfactory text, because some of the relatively important scenes were cut and various new passages added, possibly by Shakespeare himself. He also mentions that the Hecate scenes were probably written by another playwright, Thomas Middleton (1580–1627). Kelemina accepts the suggestion often made by English literary historians, namely that Shakespeare probably wrote the play ten years before its publication, already in 1605–06. He does not mention though that it may have been performed in Edinburgh, to where Shakespeare had fled after the Essex rebellion. It is generally accepted that the first public performance of this play was in London's Globe Theatre on 20 April 1611. As the immediate source for the historical background which Shakespeare used for *Macbeth* Kelemina mentions Raphael Holinshed's *Chronicles of England, Scotland, and Ireland* (1577), although Shakespeare probably used the second edition from 1587, which is more complete than the earlier one. Kelemina also mentions two other relevant sources both dealing with supernatural beings. These are Reginald Scot's famous work *The Discovery of Witchcraft* (1584) and *Daemonologie* (1597), written by James VI of Scotland, who succeeded to the English throne after the death of Queen Elizabeth I in 1603, as James I. We can see that Kelemina was familiar with all the relevant historical material, which is still valid today.

After making his statement that *Macbeth* "belongs to the most complete of Shakespeare's creations" (5) Kelemina points out the differences which exist between the text in Holinshed's *Chronicles* and Shakespeare's treatment of characters. In *Chronicles* the main hero is presented from the very beginning as an arrogant, conceited and revengeful person, whereas Shakespeare depicts Macbeth at first as a proud, heroic character, who then develops into an evil man. In Holinshed's history Lady Macbeth does not have such an important role as in Shakespeare's play, so that the psychological development of both major characters can be wholly attributed to Shakespeare. Another major difference between the plot about Macbeth and his wife is the telescoped time scale in the play: Shakespeare condensed the events which are in the legendary ("historical") account spread through twelve years of Macbeth's reign, into a much shorter period, into a few important, selected scenes. Thus Shakespeare preserved the unity of composition and created a dramatic tension which is very significant for the play.

Kelemina sees the role of the witches and demons in agreement with people's belief in such supernatural beings still common in Shakespeare's time. These creatures symbolize, in the opinion of the critic, evil forces in nature and in man. The only person in the play who is independent and who does not allow evil forces abiding in man's soul to dominate his mind, is Banquo. Kelemina believes that this indicates the playwright's persuasion that witches (man's evil nature) cannot absolutely prevail in life, although the outcome of such a decision is not necessarily positive for the hero (in this case for Banquo). Another explanation of the hero is that he is aware right from the beginning that his actions are criminal, but he is too weak to oppose decisions made by his wife. The portrait of Lady Macbeth is generally interpreted either as that of an ambitious, but loving wife, or as a brutal, egotistic person, whose negative energy exerts disastrous consequences on her husband's heroic nature (13). This is the reason, in Kelemina's view, that the reader may not completely lose his sympathy for this character. However, in this play the hero's insult of God's and nature's order is suppressed. Macbeth's tragedy is caused by the fact that he cannot decide between "man's fate" as prophesied by the witches, and the trust in his own mind and in the ethical norms of society. It seems that Kelemina underestimates the complex nature of Lady Macbeth, who mentally (and also sexually) dominates her husband and whose role in Macbeth's decision is generally viewed as more important than that in Kelemina's interpretation.

In the introduction to the play Kelemina strongly advocates his belief that Shakespeare expresses in this tragedy the idea how "some higher justice" is finally victorious in life although lives of innocent people (like Banquo) may be sacrificed in this battle between good and evil. The decisions about man's actions are left to each individual separately, depending on his character and his personal integrity, although social, political and other circumstances should also be taken into account when important decisions are at stake. It is obvious that Kelemina was particularly interested in the ethical implications of this play, and even if we may occasionally disagree with some points made in his interpretation, his essay is written in such a provocative manner that we are still intrigued by his thoughts, especially by his persuasion that the play will revive our belief "in higher justice, which cannot be deceived" (16). Kelemina compares the drama of innocent victims, caused by the cruelty of man's nature and his soul to "an apocalyptic vision of a storm or a vulcano," which have in this play been captured by the poet's imagination. In this connection Kelemina uses an image from nature according to which the idea of final justice is like "the star" showing the way to the future development of mankind. In spite of difficult tests which man has to endure in life Kelemina believes that mankind should be led into the future with the assurance of each new work of art expressing such positive ideals.

This optimism expressed in Kelemina's belief that one's life-course may depend on one's own endeavours to make life bearable as well as on one's Fate is reflected in his experiences in life. Although he was enrolled in the Austrian army at the time of the First World War, he was lucky enough not to be sent to the front line, to the Isonzo (Soča) battlefield, where so many young Slovene men died. Then, during the Second World War, he was already taken as a hostage by the German army in Kostanjevica, in Slovenia, but fortunately, he was not executed. And paradoxically enough, after the Second World War Kelemina was, as a suspected anglophile, sent to jail by the Yugoslav Communist regime, but after a few weeks of imprisonment he was released. It is also typical of Kelemina's character and his views on life that in spite of various trials he looked upon life stoically, occasionally with slightly embittered or ironic view, but essentially with positive feelings, what can also be seen from his interpretation of the above discussed macabre situations in Shakespeare's *Macbeth*. One can accept the view expressed by Janez Stanonik in his article on Kelemina that "he was a restrained character but a very kind-hearted man... whose feelings were deeply hurt by an offensive word to which he was sometimes exposed."[6] In spite of many difficulties with which he was faced in his boyhood and in his adult life Kelemina succeeded to preserve his optimistic view on life and his personal integrity.

It seems that after what has been said above the question why Kelemina stopped writing book reviews and articles about Shakespeare in 1922 can be answered with some certainty. We can see from Kelemina's remarks regarding Oton Župančič's translations, from the correspondence between Kelemina and Župančič, and also from Kelemina's correspondence with Fran Albreht that Kelemina's and Župančič's views about Župančič's translations of Shakespeare's plays were at times quite different. Although Kelemina thought highly of Oton Župančič's lyrical gift, he stated in his reviews several times that Župančič did not always catch the complex meaning and connotations implied in Shakespeare's rich figurative language. Župančič's use of his local dialect from the region of Bela Krajina, where the poet was born and spent his youth, was occasionally in opposition to the standard Slovene language. Kelemina also made in his reviews various suggestions about words and passages used in Župančič's translation, which also indicates that Kelemina did not always agree with solutions offered by Župančič in his translations. However, this does not necessarily mean that Kelemina provided a better poetic solution. According to Kelemina the translation comes closest to its perfection if the translator succeeds not only in transferring from the source language to the target language the poetic form of the original text in all of its aspects (e.g. that there is the same number of lines in the original and in the translation, the same kind of rhythm, figurative language, rhymes etc.), but when the translator also captures in the translation the greatest possible degree of the meaning expressed in the source language.[7] This is undoubtedly a demand which is still valid today. But as has already been indicated above translating from one language into another is a very complex and

---

6   Stanonik, "Jakob Kelemina", p. 334.
7   Jakob Kelemina, "Shakespeare William, *Othello,* mletački crnac". *Ljubljanski zvon* 39 (1919): pp. 761–763.

a difficult task, and sometimes it may even be impossible for a translator to perform this duty in the utmost degree due to different natures of both languages in question (e.g. the number of monosyllabic words in Slovene is much smaller than it is in English). Besides, translations do not depend only on the translator's knowledge of both languages, but also on the vocabulary and style of the language into which a text is translated as well as on the translator's linguistic ability to perform his task well. With regard to Župančič's translation of Shakespeare's plays several critics have observed that he did not adequately transmit various layers of the original text spoken by individual characters in English into the corresponding level of the Slovene. Besides, he did not always capture the patina of the original. Critics who have reviewed Župančič's translations, including Kelemina, praise Župančič's poetic gift, which is also seen in the poetic language and imagery which he used in his own poetry. On the other hand, we can also agree with Kelemina that in Slovene translations of Shakespeare's plays prepared by Župančič differences representing the social and cultural habitat of Shakespeare's characters do not always match the original. This feature can also be endorsed if we compare Župančič's translations of Shakespeare's plays and translations prepared in the following decades by Matej Bor and Milan Jesih. Their translations are – regarding the meaning of the text – closer to the original than Župančič's translations. Bor and Jesih also more frequently transplant into Slovene the colloquial type of language used by some of Shakespeare's characters than Župančič.

Conclusion

Our analysis of Kelemina's writing on Shakespeare has shown that Kelemina was basically more interested in literary, historical, ethical, and linguistic explanations of the text than in the very process of translation. In his article on Anton Funtek's, Oton Župančič's and Matej Bor's translations of *King Lear* Velimir Gjurin asserts that although Župančič corrected thirty mistakes in lexicology, grammar, idioms, made by Funtek, he committed a dozen of his own mistakes.[8] Gjurin considers the weakest

---

8   Velimir Gjurin, "Semantic Inaccuracies in Three Slovene Translations of *King Lear.*" *Acta Neophilologica* (1976): p. 83.

point of Funtek's and Župančič's translations their lack of knowledge of Shakespearean vocabulary, a fact, which was also mentioned by Kelemina in several of his writings. The main differences between Župančič and Kelemina can be found in their different approach to the text: Župančič looked upon it as a poet and translator and Kelemina as a scholar. But there is no doubt that Župančič profited from Kelemina's professional advice. Unfortunately, Župančič's translations that followed the publication of the above mentioned plays by 1939 did not have either an introduction or notes to the play and were thus "robbed" of a useful cohabitation between the work of art and a critical judgment. Two main Slovene translators of Shakespeare's plays, who continued Župančič's work, are Matej Bor and Milan Jesih. Some corrections of Župančič's translations were also made by Janko Moder, who modernized Župančič's spelling, corrected some of printer's errors, and also changed some of the archaic or dialectal words with contemporary vocabulary. However, a lot of work was still left to Matej Bor, who translated into Slovene about half of Shakespeare's plays, which had not been translated earlier. An even more radical change was made by Milan Jesih, who has so far newly translated into Slovene one third of plays written by Shakespeare. By 1990, fifty years after Župančič had translated *Romeo and Juliet*, Jesih introduced in his translations of Shakespeare's plays many changes in vocabulary, style, semantics and poetic elements. In Jesih's translation obsolete (archaic) words, which are no longer used in everyday speech are substituted with new, collo-quial expressions and idioms. He also included parts of lines which were omitted by Župančič and corrected his mistranslations.

Matej Bor, who was also the first editor of complete Shakespeare's plays in Slovene translation, admits that he began reading Shakespeare's works in Slovene translations because he was thrilled by Oton Župančič's words "which were sometimes so glittering that they even disturbed/the playwright's view of the world."[9] Bor sees the advantage of the Slovene language, if compared with some other European languages, in the fact that Slovene vocabulary is rich enough to include words that bear the stress on

---

9   Matej Bor, "Mojstri poustvarjalne besede. Matej Bor." *Zbornik Društva slovenskih književnih prevajalcev*. Ed. Frane Jerman et al. (Ljubljana: Društvo slovenskih književnih prevajalcev, 1988), p. 152.

different syllables, which makes it possible for Slovene translators to use all metrical forms, from hexameter to blank verse. One of the reasons why Bor enjoyed translating Shakespeare's plays was that this task gave him the possibility to move from his own world to a different world presented by Shakespeare. Similarly, the poet, translator and playwright Milan Jesih, sees the achievement of Oton Župančič's translations of Shakespeare's plays in his high, masterful standards of translating the English verse into Slovene, in Župančič's "effort, extending maybe even to exhibitionism, to make his language most lyrical and poetic."[10] Like other translators and critics, Jesih admires Župančič as a master "who established the standards of translating verse" into Slovene (Janez Menart). He translated Shakespeare's sonnets and other poems into Slovene, also joined Slovene translators in his praise of Župančič's translations of Shakespeare's plays.[11] However, among "weaknesses" which appear in Župančič's translations he mentions Župančič's use of Croatian words, his use of nonstandard Slovene words (corrupted variants), of archaic words and his lax neologisms. He also points out Župančič's occasional omissions of the original text. In Menart's view these features are mainly the result of the translator's wish to preserve in his translation the original rhythmic pattern and the rhyme scheme. However, Menart states that Župančič's translations are an enormous contribution to Slovene translations of Shakespeare's plays in which the translator's impact is also visible in his own style. In one way or another these views support the theses expressed by Jakob Kelemina's articles on Oton Župančič's translations of Shakespeare's plays. Although Župančič did not accept some of Kelemina's suggestions connected with his explanations of the meaning of words or idioms, Kelemina definitely contributed to Župančič's increased awareness of the linguistic complexity of Shakespeare's plays. Kelemina's studies also represent an important step in the development of Slovene criticism of Shakespeare's plays.

---

10 Milan Jesih. "Milan Jesih o svojem prevodu *Romea in Julije.*" *Zbornik Društva slovenskih književnih prevajalcev.* Ed. Aleš Berger et al. (Ljubljana: Društvo slovenskih književnih prevajalcev, 1991), p. 96.
11 Janez Menart. "Nekaj misli o Župančičevih prevodih Shakespearovih dram." *Zbornik Društva slovenskih književnih prevajalcev.* (Koper: Založba Lipa, 1980), pp. 88–92.

The author of the present study, Professsor Mirko Jurak (1935–2014), was for many years soon after World War Two the only university teacher of Shakespeare in Slovenia at the University of Ljubljana and its Faculty of Arts (cf. Jurak 2005). The study was in its longer version published in the journal *Acta neophilologica*, where he acted as Editor-in-Chief for several decades (No. 40, 2007, pp. 5–49), and was edited for publication here by Professor Igor Maver, the new editor of the journal.

Bibliography

Bezlaj, France. "Ob sedemdesetletnici profesorja Jakoba Kelermine." *Slavistična revija* 5–8, 1954, pp. 275–279.

Bor, Matej. "Mojstri poustvarjalne besede. Matej Bor." *Zbornik Društva slovenskih književnikov*. Ed. Matej Bor. "Mojstri poustvarjalne besede. Matej Bor." *Zbornik Društva slovenskih književnih prevajalcev*. Eds. Frane Jerman et al. Ljubljana: Društvo slovenskih književnih prevajalcev, 1988, pp. 152–154.

Copeland, Fanny S. "0 Župančičevih prevodih Shakespearja." *Ljubljanski zvon*, 1926, pp. 161–171.

Gjurin, Velimir. "Semantic Inaccuracies in Three Slovene Translations of *King Lear*." *Acta Neophilologica* 9, 1976, pp. 59–83.

Grošelj, Nada. "Two 17th Century Jesuit Plays in Ljubljana Inspired by English Literature." *Acta Neophilologica* 37. 1–2, 2004, pp. 61–71.

Janko, Anton. "Germanist Jakob Kelernina." *Slavistična revija* 42. 2–3, 1994, pp. 407–415.

Jesih, Milan. "Milan Jesih o svojem prevodu *Romea in Julije*." *Zbornik Društva slovenskih književnih prevajalcev*. Eds. Aleš Berger et al. Ljubljana: Društvo slovenskih književnih prevajalcev, 1991, pp. 95–103.

Jurak, Mirko. "Some Additional Notes on Shakespeare. His Great Tragedies from a Slovene Perspective." *Acta Neophilologica* 38. 1–2, 2005, 3–48.

Kelemina, Jakob. "Uvod. Opazke." William Shakespeare. *Macbeth*. Trans. Oton Župančič. Ljubljana: Tiskovna zadruga, 1921, pp. 5–16, 137–151.

Ludvik, Dušan. *Nemško gledališče v Ljubljani*. Ljubljana: Filozofska fakulteta Univerze v Ljubljani, 1957, pp. 17–19.

Menart, Janez. "Nekaj misli o Župančičevih prevodih Shakespearovih dram." *Zbornik Društva slovenskih književnih prevajalcev.* Koper: Založba Lipa, 1980, pp. 88–92.

Moravec, Dušan. "Shakespeare pri Slovencih." *W. Shakespeare. Zbrana dela.* Ed. Matej Bor. Ljubljana: Državna založba Slovenije, 1974.

Shakespeare, William. *Macbeth.* Trans. Oton Župančič. Introd. Jakob Kelemina. Ljubljana: Tiskovna Zadruga, 1921.

Stanonik, Janez. "Jakob Kelemina." *Pomurski zbornik.* Murska Sobota: Pomurska založba, 1966, pp. 332–334.

Škerlj, Stanko. *Italijansko gledališče v Ljubljani v preteklih stoletjih.* Ljubljana: Slovenska akademija znanosti in umetnosti, 1973.

Župančič, Oton. *Zbrano delo.* 12 vols. Eds. Josip Vidmar, Dušan Pirjevec, Joža Mahnič. Ljubljana: Državna založba Slovenije, 1956–1992.